**Asia Pacific Confidence and
Security Building Measures**

Significant Issues Series

SIGNIFICANT ISSUES SERIES papers are written for and published by the Center for Strategic and International Studies.

Series Editors:	David M. Abshire
	Douglas M. Johnston
Director of Studies:	Erik R. Peterson
Director of Publications:	Nancy B. Eddy
Managing Editor:	Roberta L. Howard
Associate Editor:	Yoma Ullman

The Center for Strategic and International Studies (CSIS), founded in 1962, is an independent, tax-exempt, public policy research institution based in Washington, D.C. The mission of the Center is to advance the understanding of emerging world issues in the areas of international economics, politics, security, and business. It does so by providing a strategic perspective to decision makers that is integrative in nature, international in scope, anticipatory in its timing, and bipartisan in its approach. The Center's commitment is to serve the common interests and values of the United States and other countries around the world that support representative government and the rule of law.

CSIS, as a public policy research institution, does not take specific policy positions. Accordingly, all views, positions, and conclusions expressed in this publication should be understood to be solely those of the authors.

❖   ❖   ❖

Based in Honolulu, the Pacific Forum CSIS operates as the autonomous Asia-Pacific arm of CSIS. Founded in 1975, the thrust of the Forum's work is to help develop cooperative policies in the Asia-Pacific region through debate and analyses undertaken with the region's leaders in the academic, government, and corporate arenas. The Forum collaborates with a network of more than 30 research institutes around the Pacific Rim, drawing on Asian perspectives and disseminating its projects' findings and recommendations to opinion leaders, governments, and publics throughout the region.

The Center for Strategic and International Studies
1800 K Street, N.W.
Washington, D.C.   20006
Telephone: (202) 887-0200
Fax: (202) 775-3199

Asia Pacific Confidence and Security Building Measures

Ralph A. Cossa, editor

THE CENTER FOR STRATEGIC & INTERNATIONAL STUDIES
Washington, D.C.

Cover design by Meadows and Wiser.

Significant Issues Series, Volume XVII, Number 3
© 1995 by The Center for Strategic and International Studies
Washington, D.C. 20006
Printed on recycled paper in the United States of America

99   98   97   96   95   5   4   3   2   1

ISSN 0736-7136
ISBN 0-89206-307-6

Library of Congress Cataloging-in-Publication Data

Asia Pacific confidence and security building measures   /   [edited
    by] Ralph A. Cossa.
        p. cm. — (Significant issues series, ISSN 0736-7136 ; v. 17, no. 3)
    ISBN 0-89206-307-6
      1. Asia—Politics and government—1945–   2. Pacific Area—
    Politics and government.   3. National security—Asia.   4.
    National security—Pacific Area.   I. Cossa, Ralph A.   II.
    Series.
    DS35.2.A7977   1995
    327.1'7'095—dc20   95-12882
                                                                   CIP

Contents

About the Contributors

Ralph A. Cossa is executive director of the Pacific Forum CSIS in Honolulu. He is also executive director of the U.S. Committee of the Council for Security Cooperation in the Asia Pacific (US-CSCAP). He helps direct the efforts of the multinational CSCAP Working Group on Confidence and Security Building Measures (CSBMs) in the Asia Pacific.

Kwa Chong Guan is vice chairman of the Singapore Institute of International Affairs and head of the Department of Strategic Studies at the Singapore Armed Forces Training Institute. He served previously as a policy analyst in the Singapore Ministry of Defence and as a foreign affairs officer.

Liu Huaqiu is a senior fellow and director of the Program on Arms Control and Disarmament at the China Defense Science and Technology Information Center in Beijing, which is subordinated to the Commission of Science, Technology, and Industry for National Defense of the People's Republic of China. During 1986–1987, he was a visiting fellow at the Center for International Security and Arms Control at Stanford University.

Robert A. Manning is a senior fellow at the Progressive Policy Institute in Washington, D.C., and a research associate at the Sigur Center for East Asian Studies of George Washington University. From 1989 to 1993, he was adviser for policy to the U.S. assistant secretary of state for East Asian and Pacific affairs.

Margaret (Peggy) Mason is an external fellow at the Centre for International and Strategic Studies in Toronto. She is a member of the United Nations Secretary General's Advisory Board on Disarmament Matters and chairs a UN Group of Governmental Experts study on verification. From 1989 to 1994 she was Canada's ambassador for disarmament.

Oh Kwan-chi is a senior research fellow and former vice president of the Korea Institute for Defense Analysis in Seoul. He previously served as director of KIDA's Arms Control Research Center. He is a retired Republic of Korea Army colonel.

M. Susan Pederson is assistant vice president and manager of the Programs and Policy Division of the Science Applications International Corporation in McLean, Virginia. She was formerly a member of U.S. delegations to the Conference on Security and Cooperation in Europe.

Brad Roberts is a research fellow at the Center for Strategic and International Studies in Washington, D.C., where he also serves as editor of *The Washington Quarterly.* He is cochair of the USCS-CAP CSBM task force.

Robert Ross is an associate professor at Boston University and a research associate at the John King Fairbank Center for East Asia Research at Harvard University. He is cochair of the USCSCAP CSBM task force. He is currently a visiting professor at the College of Foreign Affairs in Beijing.

Stanley Weeks is a senior scientist with the Science Applications International Corporation in McLean, Virginia, and a member of the UN Maritime Experts Group. He acted as a military consultant and naval analyst for CBS News during the 1991 Gulf War.

Preface

Until recently, multilateral approaches to confidence building in the Asia Pacific region or to regional security issues in general were resisted by the United States and most of its Asia Pacific neighbors. In the past two years, however, attitudes have changed significantly. The Council for Security Cooperation in the Asia Pacific (CSCAP) has been at the forefront of this change.

CSCAP is a multilateral, nongovernmental organization that links regional security-oriented research institutes and, through them, broad-based member committees composed of academicians, business executives, security specialists, and former and current foreign ministry and defense officials. The Pacific Forum CSIS is one of CSCAP's founding institutions and has taken the lead in establishing the U.S. Member Committee (USCSCAP).

CSCAP's research effort is accomplished through international working groups focused on specific security-related issues. The first working group to be implemented was a Confidence and Security Building Measures (CSBM) Working Group, cochaired by the U.S., Singapore, and Republic of Korea member committees. This volume provides a summation of many of the key points and insights that emerged during the first meeting of the CSCAP CSBM Working Group in Washington, D.C., in October 1994, along with updated versions of all the papers presented during the meeting.

The results of this conference were previously summarized in a Pacific Forum CSIS Policy Report entitled "Confidence and Security Building Measures: Are They Appropriate for Asia?" Chapter 1 of this volume provides a modified version of this preliminary report and summarizes the key points of both the seminar presentations and the discussions that ensued from them. Although it is hoped that most, if not all, Working Group participants would agree with the general thrust of this introductory chapter, ultimately it contains the author's own observations and interpretations, which do not necessarily represent the collective or unanimous views of the seminar attendees or participating CSCAP member committees.

The Working Group assumed that some broad-based agreement regarding the nature of the challenges confronting the Asia Pacific was a prerequisite for developing regional confidence and security building measures. Of particular importance were the differing attitudes within the region toward the nature of potential challenges. Chapters 2 through 4 provide varying perspectives on the current security environment and likely future challenges to regional stability.

In chapter 2, Robert Manning offers an American perspective. He outlines immediate, primary, and secondary U.S. concerns and disquieting regional trends. Manning focuses particular attention on three major long-term concerns: whither China? Japan's future role and direction; and the future U.S. commitment to Asia. He also looks at potentially significant nontraditional security concerns, such as piracy, environmental degradation, refugee flows, and drug trafficking.

In chapter 3, Oh Kwan-chi provides a Northeast Asia perspective. Oh concentrates on the sources of regional anxiety and the security concerns that emerge from them. These concerns include misgivings about possible new conflict on the Korean peninsula, the jeopardy of nuclear proliferation, apprehensions about the nature of any future regional security order, insecurity about the regional economic and trading system, and uneasiness over emerging nontraditional security issues. His commentary also underscores the deep suspicions that remain in South Korea over North Korean intentions, especially as regards the development of nuclear weapons—the Geneva "Agreed Framework" accord notwithstanding.

In his chapter 4 view of the security environment from the perspective of Southeast Asia or the Association of Southeast Asian Nations (ASEAN), Kwa Chong Guan takes a somewhat different approach. Kwa views the security environment through the lens of its inhabitants' social memories, providing valuable insights into how Southeast Asians view China, Japan, and the United States in particular. The past actions of all three states evoke varying levels of concern throughout Southeast Asia. Kwa cautions, however, that these mind-sets, formed during the cold war and earlier, must not prevent us from moving forward in our search for new forms of security cooperation structured around regional CSBMs.

In chapter 5, Susan Pederson and Stanley Weeks provide a comprehensive review of CSBMs worldwide. They look at CSBMs as falling into three broad categories: *declaratory measures*—statements of intent, including broad commitments such as non-attack or no-first-use agreements; *transparency measures*—including information, communication, notification, and observation/inspection measures; and *constraint measures*—including risk reduction regimes and exclusion/separation zones, as well as more traditional constraints on personnel, equipment, and operational activities. The chapter surveys all three categories of CSBMs in detail.

Ambassador Peggy Mason, in chapter 6, offers the benefit of her extensive experience working with CSBMs at the United Nations (UN) and elsewhere, while providing insights into the "real lessons" from the European CSBM experience. She examines the regional role of the UN and the normative framework it brings to the table, a framework that she fears—and illustrates—is being undermined.

In chapter 7, Liu Huaqiu provides a Chinese perspective on the topic of CSBMs, along with a list of recommended measures that seem worthy of serious study in the Asia Pacific region. Liu's chapter also articulates the many positive steps China has taken to defuse tensions and promote confidence building in recent years. This exposition of Chinese attitudes and actions provides a counterbalance to many of the concerns expressed by the other authors (and reinforced by many seminar participants) regarding current Chinese activities and long-term motives and intentions.

In the final chapter, Brad Roberts and Robert Ross summarize the analysis and recommendations developed during the USCSCAP CSBM task force's parallel investigation of this topic. Their task force report includes an extensive, extremely ambitious list of potential Asia Pacific CSBMs. This listing provided a central basis of discussion during the October 1994 meeting of the CSCAP CSBM Working Group. Recommendations in chapter 1 of this volume draw heavily from this list but are tempered by the views of the international participants.

This volume would not have been possible without the strong support of individuals too numerous to mention. At the risk of offending the many, let me highlight the contributions of a few who provided exceptional support. I am particularly grateful to Carole Penrose and Georgette Guerrero for their patience, fortitude, and outstanding administrative support, and to Brad Roberts, Jim Rutherford, and Janet Davis for all their help in arranging the various USCSCAP and CSCAP meetings that preceded this volume.

The Pacific Forum CSIS is grateful to the Asia Foundation, the Ford Foundation, the Rockefeller Brothers Fund, and the United States Institute of Peace for their generous support of this project and of CSCAP/USCSCAP activities in general. In addition, all CSCAP members remain grateful for the previous support provided by The Pew Charitable Trusts during the multinational organization's embryonic stage.

Finally, thanks to the contributing authors, not only for finding time in their schedules to prepare and then update their papers, but also for stimulating the discussion and sharpening the debate over the applicability of confidence and security building measures to the Asia Pacific region.

1

Asia Pacific Confidence and Security Building Measures

Ralph A. Cossa

Attitudes in the Asia Pacific region—particularly among members of the Association of Southeast Asian Nations (ASEAN)—regarding the acceptability or applicability of confidence and security building measures (CSBMs) appear to be changing. In July 1994, the Chairman's Statement issued at the conclusion of the inaugural ASEAN Regional Forum (ARF) meeting called for greater study of confidence and security building in the Asia Pacific.[1] The Council for Security Cooperation in the Asia Pacific (CSCAP), a nongovernmental grouping of regional security-oriented research institutions, has also strongly endorsed the study of CSBMs.[2] CSCAP's first official statement, "CSCAP Memorandum No. 1: The Security of the Asia Pacific Region," issued three months before the inaugural ARF meeting, urged the ARF to consider employing this "effective mechanism" in order to promote peace and security in the region.[3]

It is becoming increasingly clear that CSBMs, properly crafted and carefully applied, are indeed appropriate to the Asia Pacific region in the post-cold war era. This chapter supports that assumption: it addresses what types of CSBMs seem most appropriate and offers recommendations as to the best methods of cooperatively pursuing them. It begins with a look at current and potential Asia Pacific security concerns in order to better understand the security environment in which Asia Pacific CSBMs may be applied.

Asia Pacific Security Concerns

The Asia Pacific region is more peaceful and prosperous today than at any time in the past century. Nonetheless, anxieties remain about its future security. Although threat perceptions and areas of concern vary, depending on subregional perspectives, some common themes emerge when potential challenges to Asian regional stability are discussed.

People's Republic of China

China represents a primary area of concern, given its massive size, its rapidly growing economy (which some fear may over-heat) and, especially, uncertainty over its impending leadership succession. Although the country is not expected to dissolve following Senior Leader Deng Xiaoping's death, any significant instances of national or provincial instability could have serious regional consequences, especially if they involve a mass migra-tion of Chinese citizens. Even if political stability is maintained, Chinese internal and external migration could present chal-lenges if economic development is not also sustained.

There is general consensus in the region that continued eco-nomic liberalization in China is positive and should be actively supported. There is no guarantee, however, that an economically strong (and militarily powerful) China will automatically be a friendly and accommodating neighbor. Chinese actions and atti-tudes regarding the Spratly Islands are viewed by many as a good litmus test or indicator of what kind of China will emerge in Asia. Thus far, the signs are not overly reassuring.

China's growing military capabilities (which seem larger to its nearby neighbors than to the United States) remain a source of apprehension, as do questions regarding China's long-term intentions—not just in the Spratlys but toward other disputed territory as well. Concerns about the influence of overseas Chi-nese in many Asian nations and apprehensions about what will ultimately constitute "greater China" generate additional fears that are rooted deep in Asian history and in the current memo-ries and perceptions that drive the worldview of many Asian states.

The challenges associated with Hong Kong's reversion and eventual reunification of Taiwan and the mainland, although rec-ognized as an "internal Chinese matter," also add to regional apprehensions because the consequences of less-than-smooth transitions will have an impact on the entire region.

Few are willing to predict that China will inevitably pose a security threat to Asia, and even fewer would endorse branding China as a potential enemy or trying to contain it or to exclude it from regional activities. Nonetheless, "when China sneezes, the rest of the region catches cold." As a result, China's future health is constantly on its neighbors' minds, and China's active participation in multilateral security dialogues and regional confidence building measures appears essential, both to facilitate China's positive interaction with its neighbors and to assuage their concerns.

Japan

The expanding role of Japan, if managed improperly or misunderstood, also has the potential of "haunting the future of Asia." Here is another area in which Asian history and more recent memories that refuse to fade contribute to regional anxieties. As a result, although Japan remains among the most transparent of Asia Pacific nations in some respects, suspicions about its long-term intentions remain.

There is little question that Japan will play an increasingly active role in the region economically, politically, and perhaps militarily. Whether this will be perceived as threatening depends on the context surrounding Japan's involvement. In this regard, the continued viability of the Japan-U.S. security alliance is generally viewed throughout the region as essential as a guarantee of Japan's good behavior. Japan's willingness to more openly confront its past, to maintain its embrace of non-nuclear principles, and to continue to focus its efforts through multilateral channels is also seen as key to limiting future anxiety.

The Korean Peninsula

The Korean peninsula represents the area of greatest current concern as well as a source of future anxiety. The current concern centers on the suspected nuclear ambitions of the Democratic People's Republic of Korea (DPRK) and the ability of the United States, in close coordination with Pyongyang's neighbors, to defuse this crisis without severely damaging long-term relations among and between all the key players. The impact of unchecked North Korean nuclear ambitions on Japan and the Republic of Korea (ROK) is also a grave concern.

The U.S.-DPRK "Agreed Framework" accord reached in Geneva in late October 1994 has the potential, if properly executed, to reduce near-term concerns. It also has the potential to create new strains between the United States and South Korea, Japan, China, and/or Russia and others, should North Korea renege or should the various involved parties develop differing opinions as to what constitutes compliance or sufficient progress for moving from one milestone to the next. Increased dialogue between the DPRK and all its neighbors, especially the ROK, appears essential.[4]

Over the long term, concerns remain about potential North Korean political and economic scenarios (sudden collapse versus soft landing) and about eventual reunification of the peninsula. A peaceful, orderly, unrushed transition is clearly preferred but is not necessarily assured, nor is it even the most likely scenario.[5]

The Future U.S. Role

Uncertainty over the future U.S. role in Asia represents another source of regional anxiety, both in the context of the Japan-U.S. security relationship and in more general terms as well. Most Asians see the United States as an important "balancer," helping to guard against the emergence of a regional hegemon. There is a growing perception in the region, however, that the interest of the United States is waning and that its power is in decline. Many concede that, because the United States is the world's sole remaining superpower, its power and influence relative to any other single regional or global state are still paramount. Nonetheless, there is little doubt that, particularly in political and economic terms, American influence today relative to American influence in years past has declined even as Asian economies have prospered and Asian political systems have come of age—in no small part due to previous American support and encouragement.

The perception of U.S. decline or lack of interest is part of a larger concern over the shape of a new post-cold war strategic order that has yet to fully emerge in Asia. It includes concern over the future role of geoeconomic forces in shaping the Asian security environment. Although economic integration appears to be a positive force for future stability, there is also the prospect of increased economic competition over resources and markets, which could encourage the establishment of rival economic blocs. There is also a growing realization that many of the future challenges in Asia will be internal to the states involved. An unyielding U.S. commitment to regional security, even if backed by the continued forward stationing of U.S. troops in Asia, will not necessarily dampen internal flames, and American political pressures for greater democracy and individual rights could fan them.

The prevailing mood in the region today is that a continued U.S. commitment to Asian security and, more specifically, the continued forward presence of American military units, is a positive force. But even given such a continued commitment, the future U.S. role must be redefined in light of changing realities in the region to ensure that neither the United States nor its Asia Pacific neighbors fall into the trap of trying to apply cold war solutions to a post-cold war environment. Both the nature of the emerging security structure in Asia and the extent of U.S. involvement in, and commitment to, this new security order remain uncertain.

Other Areas of Concern

The above is by no means an all-inclusive list of regional security concerns. Other potential problem areas involve lingering conflicting territorial claims, concerns over the proliferation of conventional weapons as well as weapons of mass destruction and their delivery systems, and areas of persistent conflict such as Cambodia or Burma. The success or failure of Russia's political and economic reforms will also affect the future security equation in the Asia Pacific, as will leadership successions in several key states.

Meanwhile, growing economic prosperity and competition invite corruption and have the potential to resurrect historic rivalries that lie just below the surface among even the closest of regional partners. The downsides of ongoing economic miracles—increased migration (a sizable portion of it illegal), acid rain and other transnational environmental concerns, graft and corruption within the private and governmental (including military) sectors, overheated or boom-bust economies and inflation (or superinflation), competition for exploitable (including human) resources, and perhaps even destabilizing trade wars, to name but a few—will add additional nontraditional security challenges.

Other potential future threats abound, particularly to the sea lanes that link the vibrant economies of Asia to one another and to the world at large. Piracy is already a problem in the South China Sea and Gulf of Thailand and promises to grow if left unattended. Acts of terrorism on the high seas, to date largely the stuff of Hollywood movies, are not unimaginable. Unilateral or multilateral attempts to prevent transit through international straits remain a perpetual problem that could worsen if ultra-religious or ultra-nationalist regimes come to power astride vital passageways. Simple congestion and resultant accidents, oil spills, and other environmental challenges also constitute a growing potential threat to the security of the sea lanes.

Note also that almost all nations living astride Asia's sea lanes are significantly improving their military capability. Off-shore power projection capabilities and antiship missile modernization programs are at the forefront of these force modernization efforts and add a new dimension to historic concerns over the security of strategic straits and maritime passage. Regional arms races, although not currently under way, can easily be ignited or fueled, especially if the pace of modernization accelerates.

Clashes based on religion, culture, or ethnicity add to the list of potential problems, as do differences of opinion over highly emotional issues such as human rights and the promotion of democracy or political reform. As the nations of the region become more pluralistic, the conduct of foreign policy will also become more challenging. Steps taken to "sell" a policy domestically in one nation may prove offensive to neighboring nations, thus creating new antagonisms or stoking old ones. As a result, although the Asia Pacific region is today enjoying a period of relative peace and tranquility, potential security challenges are likely to arise in the future.

On the other side of the equation, history has shown that confidence and security building measures that reduce the level of uncertainty and anxiety can increase trust and understanding and thus promote greater stability and prosperity in the region. Given the nature of regional uncertainty and apprehension, it also appears clear that broad-based multilateral measures, to be effective, must include the active participation of China, Japan, and the United States and possibly Russia as well.

CSBM Survey

Given the varying types of potential threats and the region's geographical, political, and cultural diversity, the question remains as to what types of CSBMs, if any, would be appropriate to the Asia Pacific in the post-cold war era. In this regard, a greater understanding as to where CSBMs have worked or failed to work in the past—and why—appears to be a prerequisite to developing a blueprint for their possible future application.

Defining CSBMs

Definitions of CSBMs vary, ranging from the very narrow (looking almost exclusively at military measures) to much broader interpretations encompassing almost anything that builds confidence. This analysis takes the middle ground. I employ an expansive definition of CSBMs as including *both formal and informal measures, whether unilateral, bilateral, or multilateral, that address, prevent, or resolve uncertainties among states, including both military and political elements.* Such measures contribute to a reduction of uncertainty, misperception, and suspicion and thus help to reduce the possibility of incidental or accidental war.

The focus is on security, broadly defined. The intent is to alleviate tension and reduce the possibility of military conflict. CSBMs help manage problems and avoid confrontations; conflict resolution mechanisms and other attempts to deal with or redress ongoing crises or acts of aggression fall outside this definition.

For the purposes of this study, measures focused primarily on economics, such as the Asia Pacific Economic Cooperation (APEC) dialogue, are not viewed as CSBMs per se, despite the realization that security broadly defined has an economic dimension and that economic mechanisms carry with them some security consequences. This is particularly true in the APEC context because its annual meeting—especially if it continues to include a heads of state gathering—can also have profound political and security consequences.

Many different terms have been used to describe CSBMs. Again, for my purposes, the term encompasses or embraces the spirit and intent of proposals calling for trust building measures, mutual assurance measures, mutual reassurance measures, community building measures, and other related confidence building concepts.

General Observations

No attempt will be made here to chronicle all the various CSBMs that have been tried in Asia and elsewhere.[6] Instead, in an attempt to derive some pointers for the future, this section will focus on common denominators that have led to success or failure.

- *CSBMs cannot work in the absence of a desire on the part of participants to cooperate.*   There must be a general awareness among participants that the benefits to be gained outweigh both the risks associated with cooperation and the unilateral advantages to be gained by not cooperating. *CSBMs must be viewed in "win-win," not "win-lose," terms.*

- *CSBMs are most effective if they build upon or are guided by regional (and global) norms.*   They must be suited to the strategic realities and cultures that prevail in the region and in tune with the underlying political, economic, and cultural dynamism of the region in which they are being applied.

- *Foreign models do not necessarily apply.*   Most measures are highly situation dependent and require extensive tailoring. Even widely tested "universal" models may prove unworkable, especially if an attempt is made to impose them from outside the region.

- *CSBMs are stepping stones or building blocks, not institutions.* They represent means toward an end. By helping lay the groundwork, however, they may serve as useful preconditions for effective institution building.

- *CSBMs should have realistic, pragmatic, clearly defined objectives.*   Objectives should be measurable and there should be common agreement as to what constitutes compliance and progress. Measures that overreach the political willingness of the states to implement them can become sources of contention rather than accommodation.

- *Gradual, methodical, incremental approaches seem to work best.* Long-term approaches provide greater opportunity for consensus building. Attempts to leapfrog over interim steps are generally ill-advised.

- *The process, in many instances, may be as (or more) important than the product.*   This is particularly true in the initial phases. Nonetheless, while the process of instilling habits of cooperation, in and of itself, may result in greater levels of trust and understanding over time, some progress on substantive issues must ultimately occur. *Dialogue without a defined purpose can be difficult to sustain.*

Asia Pacific CSBMs

The above observations, while describing CSBMs in general, all appear applicable to Asia Pacific measures as well. Within the Asia Pacific, preference should be given to measures that address specific security problems, take into account the unique geostrategic character and cultures of the region or subregion, relate to the prevailing stage of political accommodation among all involved actors, and build on historical and institutional experiences in the region.

Several additional observations also appear in order when specifically discussing this region. First, it should be understood that *the Asia Pacific is not itself a homogeneous region,* but rather consists of several subregions (and sub-subregions) that are unique in many respects.

Second, as a general rule, within the various Asian subregions there is a *preference for informal structures and a tendency to place greater emphasis on personal relationships* than on formal structures. Consensus building is a key prerequisite. There is also a general distrust of Western (especially European) "solutions." Even good European examples are not likely to be seriously considered, much less followed, unless the European label is removed.

Third, there is a *genuine commitment in Asia to the principle of noninterference* in the internal affairs of others. This commitment cannot be dismissed as a mere excuse to avoid living up to international commitments or observing recognized universal principles—nor should it be used for this purpose. It is also recognized that in a more interconnected world, a nation's internal developments can have broader regional, and even international, ramifications. Differences in interpretation over the external implications of internal events and over approaches aimed at achieving, measuring, or guaranteeing universal basic rights persist, however, both between and within Asia Pacific subregions.

Policy Recommendations

The prospective CSBMs that follow are presented for ease of discussion under four general headings—expand transparency measures, support global treaty regimes, build on existing cooperation, and develop new multilateral approaches—with the recognition that overlap exists among the groupings.[7]

Expand Transparency Measures

Transparency measures represent convenient, low-risk methods for promoting confidence in the near term while laying the foundation for more ambitious programs to follow. Although transparency could in some circumstances contribute to instability, in general, greater transparency about military doctrine, capabilities, and intentions can provide reassurance and help build trust and confidence.

A wide variety of military transparency measures have been tried. These include direct military-to-military contacts, visits by military delegations, military personnel exchange programs, intelligence exchange, prior notification of military exercises, the opening of military exercises to international observers, greater openness regarding military budgets and defense planning and procurement, and the preparation of defense white papers. Many have been, or could easily be, initiated unilaterally or pursued on a bilateral or multilateral basis in the region. Nongovernmental organizations (NGOs) such as CSCAP can play a useful role in the development both of minimum standards of openness and of common definitions or uniform outlines for defense white papers, arms registries, statements of defense expenditures, and other transparency measures.

There is also a need for greater dialogue on security issues both among the region's uniformed militaries and between the military and civilian communities. Greater participation by the uniformed military in security-oriented dialogue would add an important dimension to such discussions. It would facilitate more informed debate and enhance the relevancy of end products, while also increasing the level of understanding between military officers and their civilian interlocutors in both the foreign ministry and academic communities. Greater effort is needed on the part of both governmental and nongovernmental organizations to encourage and facilitate informed public debate on security issues.

The creation of a regionwide arms registry merits serious consideration, given the increased military expenditures among most of the region's nations and lingering suspicions about military capabilities and intentions. As proposed by Malaysia in

1992, a regional arms registry could provide more detailed information and entail stricter reporting requirements than the current United Nations (UN) Register of Conventional Arms. Such an effort could reduce the prospect of a spiraling arms race growing out of regional suspicions or misunderstandings about increased defense expenditures on the part of many nations in the region.

Support Global Treaty Regimes

Regional states should more actively support global arms control treaty regimes because of the benefits of confidence and security they bring to the region. Endorsement of global regimes could provide a measure of assurance that neighboring states are not about to embark on new programs of strategic significance; this, in turn, could help defuse potential regional arms races. Conversely, a failure to endorse or honor global mechanisms could demonstrate a lack of confidence in CSBMs in general and raise questions about regional willingness to embrace other such measures.

The next two years will be critical for global nonproliferation regimes dealing with unconventional weapons or weapons of mass destruction. Of particular significance is the scheduled renewal of the Nuclear Non-Proliferation Treaty (NPT). The nuclear weapon states, especially the United States, have placed high priority on the indefinite extension of the NPT when it comes up for renewal in 1995.

Most Asian nations have not focused a great deal of attention on the NPT issue and few, if any, share the U.S. sense of urgency as regards this topic. Nonetheless, it is likely to become a contentious issue in the next year, given expected U.S. pressure and Asian insistence that the nuclear "haves" convince the "have-nots" why it is in their interest to let the nuclear powers continue their exclusive club. If broad-based renewal of the NPT is to occur, the nuclear powers must clearly articulate what concrete steps they plan to take to further denuclearize the planet—and non-nuclear Asian states must make it clear what they expect from the nuclear powers in return for their support.

Other global activities or initiatives worth pursuing include measures to strengthen the Biological and Toxin Weapons Convention, the implementation of the Chemical Weapons Convention, the possible expansion of the Missile and Technology Control Regime into a global treaty, support for a Comprehensive Test Ban Treaty, universal endorsement of nuclear no-first-use policies, and enhancement of the safeguard mechanisms of the International Atomic Energy Agency (IAEA). The latter three subjects could enter into the debate on NPT renewal as well.

Build on Existing Cooperation

Patterns and habits of practical cooperation already exist on a diverse set of security-related issues within the Asia Pacific. The possibility of building upon or expanding existing mechanisms should be vigorously explored.

The expansion of existing maritime cooperation efforts into a broad-based maritime safety and security regime is an area that shows particular promise. One possible approach would be the multilateralization of the old U.S.-Soviet or recent Russian-Japanese Incidents at Sea agreements, perhaps broadened to include safety-at-sea measures as well. Measures to combat smuggling or piracy, to monitor pollution, and to provide common search and rescue or humanitarian relief capabilities should also be explored.[8]

Nuclear-weapons-free zones represent another idea whose time has finally come. Traditional U.S. reluctance to participate in such regimes appears to have diminished with the end of the cold war and the unilateral withdrawal of tactical nuclear weapons from deployed U.S. ships and military aircraft. All Asia Pacific nations—the United States specifically included—are encouraged to endorse the South Pacific Nuclear Free Zone (SPNFZ) proposal, as outlined in the Treaty of Rarotonga, recognizing that the treaty accommodates the "right of transit" and "neither confirm nor deny" principles. The advantages of a nuclear-weapons-free Korean peninsula were also recognized. Other Asia Pacific subregions may lend themselves to such zones as well.

Mutual interests in the peaceful uses of nuclear energy also provide opportunities for multilateral cooperation, with early emphasis perhaps focused on nuclear safety and regulatory issues. The 1994 Japan-ROK-Russia joint study on radioactive contamination in the North Pacific is one working example of multilateral cooperation on issues related to nuclear safety. The subject of expanding regional cooperation in the area of national export control (especially as regards dual-use technology), although sensitive and not broadly supported in the region, also appears worthy of additional consideration.

Develop New Multilateral Approaches

The time does not appear opportune for the creation of formalized governmental mechanisms to deal specifically with potential hotspots such as the Spratlys or the Korean peninsula.
Nonetheless, Indonesia's ongoing efforts to act as an honest bro-
ker in establishing a dialogue among all the various Spratly
claimants should be supported and encouraged—if not formalized—and careful consideration should be given to the ROK foreign minister's proposal at the 1994 ARF meeting for a
Northeast Asia security dialogue. Cautious, low-keyed
approaches seem best when dealing with potentially volatile
and dangerous issues.

Proposals dealing with the establishment of comprehensive
or collective security mechanisms for the Asia Pacific should also
receive careful consideration, even if a security arrangement akin
to the North Atlantic Treaty Organization (NATO) is inappropri-
ate for the region at this time.[9] The creation of a formal, comprehensive, regionwide transparency regime analogous to the
Organization for Security and Cooperation in Europe (OSCE,
formerly CSCE) is also considered neither desirable nor feasible
in the Asia Pacific in the post-cold war era.

Although many in the region do not appear ready for such
an effort, serious thought should also be given to the creation of
nongovernmental multilateral mechanisms to promote a dialogue on effective governance in order to help reduce the corrosive impact of debates over human rights and the promotion of
democracy and political pluralism. Although this is more a political than a traditional security issue, it remains a highly emotional, potentially divisive subject that bear directly on security
relationships in the Asia Pacific.

Future Steps

There are many confidence and security building measures,
especially in the transparency area, that can be initiated unilaterally, and Asia Pacific governments are encouraged to pursue
those measures consistent with their own security needs. Bilateral approaches have also proven successful in the past and
should continue, because they provide a useful model and a
solid foundation upon which to build broader-based CSBMs.

In the multilateral arena, the ARF is seen both as a political
confidence building measure in its own right and as a vehicle for

Chart 1.1
Asia Pacific CSBMs: General Observations

CSBMs cannot work in the absence of a desire on the part of participants to cooperate

CSBMs must be viewed in "win-win," not "win-lose," terms

CSBMs are most effective if they build upon or are guided by regional (and global) norms

Foreign models do not necessarily apply

CSBMs are stepping stones or building blocks, not institutions

CSBMs should have realistic, pragmatic, clearly defined objectives

Gradual, methodical, incremental approaches seem to work best

The process, in many instances, may be as (or more) important than the product

Dialogue without a defined purpose can be difficult to sustain

As regards Asia Pacific CSBMs in particular, it should be remembered that

- the Asia Pacific is not itself a homogeneous region
- there is a preference for informal structures and a tendency to place greater emphasis on personal relationships
- consensus building is a key prerequisite
- there is general distrust of outside "solutions"
- there is genuine commitment to the principle of noninterference in one another's internal affairs

---

examining and promoting Asia Pacific CSBMs. The ARF seems particularly well-suited to becoming the consolidating and validating instrument behind many security initiatives proposed by governments and NGOs in recent years. Its support of such ideas as an Asian arms registry, military transparency, and other confidence and security building measures should generate greater support for, and provide greater focus to, efforts at both the official and track two levels to develop innovative new measures for

Chart 1.2
Prospective Asia Pacific CSBMs

Expand Transparency Measures

- Broadly apply existing military transparency measures
- Produce standardized defense white papers
- Promote greater dialogue among the region's militaries
- Establish an Asian arms registry

Support Global CSBMs

- Endorse renewal of the NPT and strengthen IAEA safe-guards
- Strengthen the Biological Weapons Convention
- Implement/enforce the Chemical Weapons Convention
- Expand the MTCR into a global treaty
- Support a CTBT and no-first-use principles

Build on Existing Cooperation

- Establish a maritime safety and security regime
- Establish nuclear-weapons-free zones (especially in the South Pacific and on the Korean peninsula)
- Expand cooperation on nuclear safety/regulatory issues
- Explore dual-use technology export control regimes

Develop New Multilateral Approaches

- Formalize Indonesia's Spratly Islands initiative
- Establish Northeast Asia dialogue mechanisms
- Promote dialogues on effective governance
- Recognize that a Conference on Security and Cooperation in Asia is neither desirable nor feasible

dealing with potentially sensitive regional security issues. The research efforts being conducted by the various CSCAP Working Groups can also contribute positively to greater understanding about, and support for, regional confidence building.[10]

Progress may also be facilitated if better account is taken of developments at the global level—for example, at the UN Disarmament Commission—that have effectively "internationalized" certain broad principles in relation to confidence building and openness in military matters. In this regard, the UN-sponsored regional security dialogue activities (collectively referred to as the "Kathmandu process") should be seen as an important complement to other track two efforts. Attempts should be made to promote a mutually beneficial interaction between regional institutions and the UN in its regional role.

Conclusion

CSBMs, if properly devised and executed (in accordance with the general observations noted in chart 1.1), can promote peace and stability in the Asia Pacific. Regional states are encouraged to pursue as quickly and broadly as possible unilateral and bilateral measures that not only build trust and confidence in their own right but also help lay the foundation for broader-based regional or subregional multilateral cooperation.

Multilateral organizations such as the ASEAN Regional Forum are encouraged to place CSBMs (such as the ones contained in chart 1.2) high on their future agenda. Both the ARF and its individual members, as well as other nations and territories throughout the Asia Pacific, are encouraged to support, provide input for, and otherwise participate in CSCAP Working Group activities and other NGO and official initiatives aimed at enhancing trust and confidence and promoting security-oriented dialogue in the Asia Pacific.

To sum up, the preferred method for approaching CSBMs in the Asia Pacific region appears to be as follows: start small; take a gradual, incremental, building-block approach; recognize that European models are generally not transferable to Asia and that subregional differences exist within the Asia Pacific; apply individual CSBMs only where they fit; do not overformalize the process; and do not neglect the importance of unilateral and bilateral measures as stepping stones toward multilateral confidence building. In short, proceed slowly and carefully, but definitely proceed.

Notes

1.   The ASEAN Regional Forum is an official government-sponsored multinational organization that brings together foreign ministers from 18

Asia Pacific nations for formal discussions on regional security issues. The first ARF meeting took place in Bangkok in July 1994. Foreign ministers from Australia, Brunei, Canada, China, Indonesia, Japan, the Republic of Korea, Laos, Malaysia, New Zealand, Papua New Guinea, the Philippines, Russia, Singapore, Thailand, and Vietnam attended, as did a senior representative from the European Union. Deputy Secretary of State Strobe Talbott represented the United States.

2.   The Pacific Forum CSIS joined with nine other institutes in July 1993 in Kuala Lumpur to establish the Council for Security Cooperation in the Asia Pacific (CSCAP) as a nongovernmental forum for multilateral security dialogue. Founding CSCAP members represent institutes in Australia, Canada, Indonesia, Japan, South Korea, Malaysia, the Philippines, Singapore, Thailand, and the United States. New Zealand, North Korea, and Russia have since joined, and a consortium from the European Union and an Indian institute have been admitted as associate members. CSCAP membership is open to all countries and territories in the Asia Pacific region. CSCAP members seek to enhance regional security and stability through dialogues, consultations, and cooperation. The council also encourages and supports official dialogue on cooperative security, such as the ASEAN Regional Forum.

3.   CSCAP's international Steering Group also established an international CSBM Working Group to further investigate and promote Asia Pacific CSBMs. This chapter, and indeed the chapters that follow, represent the initial fruits of this Working Group's labor, as seen through the eyes of the respective authors.

4.   The recent entry of the DPRK into CSCAP should help facilitate this dialogue at the nongovernmental level.

5.   A separate CSCAP Working Group, cosponsored by the Canadian and Japanese member committees, has been formed to examine various frameworks for promoting long-term stability on the Korean peninsula and elsewhere in Northeast Asia.

6.   For such a listing, please see chapter 5 of this volume.

7.   Inclusion in this list implies neither unanimous support nor equal levels of enthusiasm among CSCAP CSBM Working Group participants or member committees. Most of these proposed measures were, however, generally well-received by the CSBM Working Group. A CSCAP Memorandum is currently being prepared that will provide a coordinated listing of recommendations regarding potential Asia Pacific CSBMs.

8.   A separate CSCAP Working Group, cosponsored by the Australian and Indonesian member committees, has been formed to examine the topic of maritime cooperation.

9.   A separate CSCAP Working Group, cosponsored by Malaysia and New Zealand, is investigating the concepts of cooperative security and comprehensive security and their possible relevance to, or significance for, the Asia Pacific region.

10.   For its part, the CSCAP CSBM Working Group will conduct, during the spring of 1995, a more comprehensive analysis of several of the measures highlighted above. In light of the pending debate over renewal of the

NPT in 1995, Asian participation in this and other global CSBMs was given a high priority for future study. In addition, the CSBM Working Group will further investigate military transparency measures to determine which are most suited to the Asia Pacific region. The group will also conduct an examination of the UN Register of Conventional Arms and the feasibility and desirability of developing an expanded, more detailed Asian arms registry.

2

Building Community or Building Conflict? A Typology of Asia Pacific Security Challenges

Robert A. Manning

Amid the rise of China and Japan as multidimensional great powers and considerable uncertainty about the meaning of that emerging reality, an Asia in the throes of generational leadership change, flushed with self-confidence from its enviable economic success, is in the process of defining its post-cold war interests and institutions to safeguard its economic growth and ameliorate its security concerns. Although the cold war furnished the overriding rationale for the U.S. security presence in Asia, it was regional concerns that largely motivated—and continue to motivate—local actors to form and sustain the set of bilateral U.S. alliances that have been an informal core security framework in the region. Indeed, Asia was sobered by the example of Leninist states in hot and cold nationalist conflict with each other: Sino-Soviet, Sino-Vietnamese, and Vietnamese-Khmer.

There was always a second dimension to the U.S. security presence, that of regional balancer, a role that now serves as its primary rationale.[1] The current security environment is marked by a modestly reduced U.S. military role (and widespread East Asian assumptions that it will continue to diminish, if incrementally), the growing military capabilities of virtually all actors in the region, and an unparalleled economic dynamism in which intra-Asian and transpacific trade and investment have grown exponentially in the two decades since the Vietnam War. This rise of geoeconomics must be considered an important, if not decisive, integrative factor reshaping the long-term security calculus of regional actors. Yet, the Asia Pacific region is characterized by what the Chinese might call the three contradictions:

- It is more prosperous and peaceful than at any time in the past century, yet haunted by its past and uneasy about the future.

- Apart from the North Korean nuclear threat and tensions on the Korean peninsula there are no immediate security threats, yet the region features the world's largest military forces—and most Asian states continue to increase their military spending even as the United States, Russia, and the European states reduce theirs.

- In an age when regional economic integration is rapidly increasing and instantaneous global flows of capital and information have eroded the very concept of sovereignty, long-standing territorial disputes are becoming more prominent.

Security Challenges

Embodied within these contradictions are several categories of security challenges. There are immediate, primary concerns such as war, instability, or a new regional nuclear arms race resulting from events on the Korean peninsula. Then there are three major long-term concerns: whither China? Japan's future role and direction; and the future U.S. commitment to Asia. There are also secondary concerns, typified by the Spratly Islands dispute and China-Taiwan tensions, and tertiary disputes, such as conflicting claims over Sipidan and Ligatan or over the Senkaku Islands. Moreover, there are latent and amorphous historic fears, suspicions, and rivalries that could potentially become major sources of instability.

In addition, there are disquieting trends such as increased military spending and force modernization along with the possibility of internal strife in several nations, including the still remote, but not inconceivable, possibility of resurgent Islamic fundamentalism in Southeast and Central Asia. Finally, there are significant nontraditional security concerns, such as piracy, environmental degradation, refugee flows, and drug trafficking.

The Korean Question

The principal—and immediate—source of tension most likely to result in instability or conflict is the heavily armed standoff on the Korean peninsula. The most urgent issue is the North Korean nuclear weapons program; the longer-term concern is the process of Korean reunification. Both have global proliferation, as well as regional security, aspects. Although discussion of the global aspects is beyond the scope of this chapter, North Korea's threat to leave the Nuclear Non-Proliferation Treaty (NPT) and the precedent of an NPT member state out of compliance with obligations imposed by the International Atomic Energy Agency (IAEA) are unsettling realities as the April 1995 NPT extension conference approaches. The U.S.-North Korea "Agreed Framework" accord of October 21, 1994, has frozen Pyongyang's nuclear weapons program and offers the prospect of terminating the program over the next decade as light water reactors are constructed to replace North Korea's gas-graphite reactors. But even if it is strictly implemented, the accord allows North Korea to maintain its opaque nuclear status for at least five years before Pyongyang is committed to cooperating with the IAEA in clarifying its past nuclear activities.

In regional terms, the nuclear issue is inextricably bound up in the question of Korean reunification, the scenarios for which run the spectrum from implosion and a Romania-type collapse to explosion and a second Korean war. And, because the interests of the four major powers in Northeast Asia intersect on the Korean peninsula, how reunification occurs is likely to have major implications for the regional balance, particularly for the future of the U.S. forward deployed military presence in the region.

In pondering Korean scenarios, the starting point is the best-case scenario, a "soft landing" for North Korea, the preferred choice of both North and South Korea as well as the four major powers. The possibilities for such a scenario have been enhanced by the negotiated accord for the termination of North Korea's nuclear weapons program. But ultimately this outcome rests on the willingness of a new leadership in Pyongyang to pursue Chinese-type economic reforms and to trade its nuclear program for economic and political engagement with the international community.

The theory behind the "soft landing" is that foreign trade, aid, and investment would cushion and begin to refurbish the failing North Korean economy such that a gradual, peaceful reunification process could result with help from a magnanimous Republic of Korea (ROK). Although not inconceivable, and certainly the most desirable scenario, fears of the Pyongyang leadership that even a controlled opening of the most closed society on earth would lead to their undoing suggest that such an outcome is highly problematic.

An implosion scenario could involve large flows of refugees from North Korea across the demilitarized zone (DMZ) to South

Korea, to ethnic Korean areas of China, and to Japan. Although it might be peaceful, a collapse of regime or struggle between North Korean factions could also involve military force and might be destabilizing to Northeast Asia in general, as well as to South Korea (which would bear primary responsibility for a reunification by force majeure). An explosion scenario would be one in which a desperate North Korea, sensing impending doom, launches a suicidal assault on the South, hoping to seize Seoul and then sue for peace.

In the case of either implosion or explosion the result would be a rapid unification by absorption. Such an outcome would resolve the nuclear issue (although in a worst case it could lead to a Ukraine-type problem of inherited nuclear capability). This could have a palliative effect on a prospective subregional Northeast Asia nuclear arms race—the specter of which has been greatly exaggerated in Western commentaries. Korean nuclear proliferation has not been a factor in Chinese nuclear modernization plans, and Japan, which has lived with hundreds of Chinese bombs, will not abandon its constitution or pacifist political culture, certainly not in the near term, because Pyongyang proliferates. But North Korea provides political cover for Japanese development of high-tech dual-use capabilities (from accumulating plutonium to the H-2 rocket) and defensive systems designed, in no small measure, with China in mind. A muddle-through scenario in which North Korea destroys its history and achieves opaque nuclear status, while covertly enhancing its nuclear and missile capabilities, would perpetuate this reality.

Any German-type reunification would lead to a reassessment of the U.S. troop presence in Korea. Although some in U.S. and ROK defense circles envision an as yet unspecified regional role for the United States in Korea, it is at best highly problematic whether a U.S. forward troop presence would be politically sustainable domestically for very long after a stable, reunified Korea takes shape—unless China becomes widely perceived as an adversary, as was the USSR.[2] A U.S. withdrawal from Korea would, in turn, put new pressures to reduce, and certainly restructure (if not reassess) the U.S. military presence in Japan, which would then be the last country hosting forward deployed U.S. bases in the Pacific outside U.S. territory. Such a dynamic could have a destabilizing impact on the East Asian balance or, at a minimum, fuel regional suspicions, altering the political-military calculus of the major actors.

South China Sea

The festering territorial disputes in the South China Sea are in some respects of a different, and perhaps more troubling, character than either the looming denouement in Korea or the plethora of unresolved sovereignty and territorial claims that are part of the Asian geopolitical landscape. In particular, the contending claims of China (and Taiwan), Vietnam, Malaysia, the Philippines, and Brunei over the Spratlys are the most likely source of armed conflict in Southeast Asia in the medium term (a time frame of 5 to 10 years). Indeed, these claims have already produced sporadic clashes between China and Vietnam, including a naval skirmish that left 72 dead in March 1988 and, most recently, a Chinese blockade of a Vietnamese oil rig in a kind of war of American concessions. Setting the stage for future clashes, Hanoi responded to Beijing's 1992 award of an oil concession overlapping with Vietnamese claims to Crestone, a U.S. firm, by awarding a similar concession to a consortium including Mobil Oil.[3]

It is widely assumed that in and around these barren rocks and islets lies a treasure trove of oil and gas resources. Yet there are precious few authoritative surveys indicating that the assumed massive quantities of resources (let alone commercially viable gas or oil) actually exist. But perception is what ultimately shapes behavior.

The current (and projected) military capabilities of the claimants suggest a time horizon that will allow several years for the employment of diplomacy before more than minor military confrontations are likely to occur. In addition, geography is likely to limit military engagement to air and naval warfare for control of the disputed areas rather than generalized conflict. But the South China Sea issue is a barometer of two key points about the emerging security environment: the degree to which capabilities can affect intentions in general, and Chinese strategic intentions in particular.

Another motivating factor behind the military buildup in the region is the Law of the Sea Treaty, which gave countries 200-mile Exclusive Economic Zones (EEZs) to protect. Thus the member states of the Association of Southeast Asian Nations (ASEAN) have been modernizing their air and naval forces in particular: Malaysia has acquired 28 Hawks, 8 F-18Ds, 18 MiG-29s, and missile frigates; Singapore, F-16s and E2Cs; Indonesia,

former East German ships; and Thailand, F-16s. Taiwan's acquisition of 60 Mirage 2000s and 150 F-16s alone dwarfs ASEAN
procurement.

Meanwhile, China's purchase of 24 Su-27s (with up to 48
more to come), their exclusive basing in the southern region
(including some on the island of Hainan), the building of a military base on Woody Island in the Paracels, the acquisition of 24
MiG-31 Foxhound interceptors, the development of air refueling
capabilities, naval modernization, and rapid deployment/local
war doctrine all point in one direction. Against the background
of China's expansive 1992 sovereignty law, and its historic pattern of using military force, Beijing's resistance to efforts to ele-
vate the Indonesian-sponsored South China Sea workshops to
official diplomacy is an issue of concern. China's pro forma participation in nascent security dialogues while impeding any serious attempts at preventive diplomacy, amid its continuing
military modernization, suggests a strategy of calculated ambiguity designed to result in an outcome on Chinese terms.

China-Taiwan

Prospective conflict between China and Taiwan is perhaps
the most intriguing near- to medium-term security challenge
because it tests the strength of geoeconomic imperatives. China-
Taiwan economic relations are mushrooming and pushing
toward integration, but politics is pulling in precisely the other
direction. From barely $500 million in trade in 1988, China-Tai-
wan trade reached $20 billion in 1993, and Taiwanese investment
in the mainland has grown to more than $15 billion (by some
estimates as much as $25 billion), with an estimated 100,000 Tai-
wanese enterprises on the mainland.[4] This is all the more
remarkable because there were no direct official economic ties or
accords at all until August 1994.[5] Moreover, at the people-to-peo-
ple level, since 1988, more than 6 million Taiwanese have visited
the mainland. This private sector dynamism has already produced policy shifts in both Beijing and Taipei, from a no contact
policy to regular high-level "official unofficial" dialogue through
respective private "foundations" created by each government,
to the August breakthrough accord aimed at addressing new
practical issues ranging from investment guarantees to cross-
straits marriages.

At the same time, Beijing has not renounced the use of force
against Taiwan if it opts for independence—and there is a significant, if not growing, movement for independence on Taiwan.

Moreover, Taipei continues to seek a higher international political profile, including efforts to gain a presence in the United
Nations (UN). This drive is animated by domestic political
dynamics, as native Taiwanese opposition forces and elements of
a Kuomintang no longer dominated by Mainlanders make their
presence felt. A remarkably effective Taiwan lobby in Washington threatens to add volatility to this combustible mix by fueling
congressional activism.

Thus, economics and politics appear to be pulling in opposite directions. The Taiwan Strait remains a potential source of
regional conflict, one that could easily lead to U.S. military
involvement. Thus far there has been incremental progress in
resolving this dilemma, such as both Beijing and Taipei attaining
membership in the Asian Development Bank and the Asia
Pacific Economic Cooperation (APEC) forum; both are also in the
process of joining the General Agreement on Tariffs and Trade
(GATT). How these competing trends play out will be an interesting measure of the degree to which geoeconomics is reshaping political behavior.

Other Territorial Issues

A broad range of other territorial disputes exist in the Asia
Pacific, as indicated in chart 2.1. These are in a different category from the disputes mentioned above because they are more
bilateral irritants than disputes likely to spark military conflict.
The potential for armed conflict is remote in these cases. Most
prominent among them are the Northern Territories dispute
between Russia and Japan and conflicting claims over the Senkaku Islands by China and Japan. In both instances, this real
estate is of little intrinsic value to any of the claimants except as
an enduring symbol of nationalism.

The Northern Territories dispute is a symbol of a century-old
Russo-Japanese enmity, embedded in the pathology of the relationship, that will only be resolved over time as nationalism
matures on both sides and is transcended by a mutual need to
remove the issue from the bilateral agenda. The Senkakus are
tangential to the Sino-Japanese relationship and it is difficult to
envision conflict over the islands, unless a climate of strategic
rivalry evolved such that they became a spark to start a fire wait-
ing to happen. Much the same could be said for the rest of the
laundry list of conflicting territorial claims, such as that between
Malaysia and Indonesia over Ligitan and Sipadan.

Chart 2.1
Sovereignty, Legitimacy, and Territorial Conflicts in East Asia

- Competing Soviet/Russian and Japanese claims to the southern Kurile Islands, referred to by the Japanese as "the Northern Territories, namely, Kunashiri, Etorofu and Shikotan Islands, an integral part of Japanese territory, illegally occupied by the Soviet Union"

- The unresolved dispute between Japan and South Korea over the Liancourt Rocks (Takeshima or Tak-do) in the southern part of the Sea of Japan

- Divided sovereignty on the Korean peninsula, where some 1.4 million ground forces of the Republic of Korea and North Korea remain deployed against each other across the demilitarized zone

- Competing sovereignty claims of the Chinese regimes on mainland China and Taiwan

- The unresolved dispute between Japan and China over the Senkaku (Diaoyutai) Islands in the East China Sea

- The armed Communist and Muslim insurgencies in the Philippines

- The continuing claim of the Philippines to the Malaysian state of Sabah and its adjacent waters

- The strong separatist movement in Sabah

- Competing claims to the Paracel Islands (Xisha Quandao or Quan Doa Hoang Sa) in the South China Sea, contested by China and Vietnam

- Competing claims to the Spratly Islands in the South China Sea, contested by China, Vietnam, Brunei, Malaysia, Taiwan, and the Philippines

- Border disputes between China and Vietnam

Chart 2.1 (continued)
Sovereignty, Legitimacy, and Territorial Conflicts in East Asia

- Boundary dispute between Indonesia and Vietnam on their demarcation line on the continental shelf in the South China Sea, near Natuna Island

- Border disputes between Vietnam and Cambodia

- Boundary dispute between Vietnam and Malaysia on their offshore demarcation line

- The Bougainville secessionist movement in Papua New Guinea

- The Organisasi Papua Merdeka (OPM) resistance movement in West Irian/Irian Jaya

- The continuing resistance to Indonesian rule in East Timor

- The Aceh independence movement in northern Sumatra

- The dispute between Malaysia and Singapore over ownership of the island of Pulau Batu Putih (Pedra Branca), some 55 km east of Singapore on the Straits of Johore

- The competing claims of Malaysia and Indonesia to the islands of Sipadan, Sebatik, and Ligitan, in the Celebes Sea, some 35 km from Semporna in Sabah

- Border dispute between Malaysia and Thailand

- Residual conflict in Cambodia

- Continued fighting between government and resistance forces in Laos

- Residual Communist guerilla operations along the Thai-Lao border in northeast Thailand

- Border conflicts between Thailand and Burma

Source: Desmond Ball, "Arms and Affluence," *International Security* 18 (winter 1993/94): 88.

Internal Instability

There are a host of instances of real and potential internal instability in East Asia, some of which may have a bearing on security considerations, and some of which are unlikely to have an external impact. There remains turmoil in Cambodia, but the external power aspect (Sino-Soviet, Sino-Vietnamese, Thai-Vietnamese) has largely disappeared, leaving it principally a civil conflict inside Cambodia. Looking ahead, the Khmer Rouge problem is most likely to become another dwindling insurgency, with some potential spillover for Thai-Vietnamese relations, although neither Bangkok nor Hanoi has demonstrated much interest in a contest for spheres of influence.

The looming passage of the 70-year-old Suharto from the Indonesian leadership scene could open up a succession/generational struggle. A dissipation of authority could in turn encourage secessionist forces in Aceh or East Timor. Although Indonesia has thus far institutionalized Islam, there is also a possibility, however slight, of an upsurge in radical Islam. This is also true across the board at a time of uncertainty and change in the Malay archipelago (Malaysia, Brunei, the Philippines), particularly if the region's economic dynamism slackens. Unless a radical Islamic upsurge sweeps the region it is difficult to see how any instability in Indonesia or elsewhere would have more than a minor impact beyond the country affected. Pressures for change on the ruling State Law and Order Restoration Council (SLORC) in Burma could also produce instability, but again, this is likely to be contained within its borders.

The one potential source of instability with major regional impact is turmoil during a difficult succession in a post-Deng China that is likely to be protracted over a period of two to three years. Although such an outcome is not the most probable, neither is it inconceivable. The combination of festering economic problems, the absence of ideological glue, and diminished authority with the end of first-generation revolutionary leadership could exacerbate trends toward regional autonomy or, in the worst case, warlordism and civil strife. Such a scenario could raise the problem of "loose nukes" or autonomous nuclear forces. Historically, the chief danger of an unstable China has been that it tends to invite outside intervention. In any case, the immediate post-Deng leadership will almost certainly view nationalism as a source of political legitimacy and will orient itself in that direction.[6]

Whither China?

Of greater concern in the region are China's intentions, whatever its political coloration or internal distribution of power. Thus far, Beijing appears to be pursuing a two-track strategy of calculated ambiguity. At one level it is integrating itself into both international and regional economic and political institutions: GATT and its successor, the World Trade Organization; the NPT; (in theory) the Missile Technology Control Regime; the APEC organization; and the ASEAN Regional Forum. Moreover, China has been cooperative, if highly idiosyncratic in operating style, on the most pressing regional security issue, the North Korean nuclear problem.[7]

At the same time, China appears intent on preserving maximum autonomy of action and continues its military modernization despite the most peaceful security environment it has enjoyed for more than a century. China's most dramatic gesture was the passage by its National People's Congress on February 25, 1992, of a Law on Territorial Waters and Contiguous Zones that proclaims Chinese sovereignty over vast swathes of the South and East China Seas. Not only does the law assert Chinese sovereignty over the Spratlys, Paracels, and Senkakus, but it defines the South China Sea in such away that even the right of passage (other than through straits) in theory requires permission from Beijing. Apart from the fact that the Chinese claims are based on questionable historical grounds, its own law is inconsistent with some provisions in the Law of the Sea Treaty, which China has signed (but not yet ratified).

Perhaps more important than the enactment of the law is the political context. The law was signed at a time of rising concern about the Spratlys and during a period (which persists) when China's defense spending had more than doubled since 1988. Moreover, China is actively acquiring force projection capabilities, such as air-refueling, a blue-water navy, and perhaps even an aircraft carrier. Chinese policy toward Burma may also be seen in this light. Beyond serving as a major arms supplier to the SLORC, China reportedly has access to a naval base at the mouth of the Irrawaddy River. China has also established a monitoring station on Burma's Coco Island and is upgrading roads and railways near and across the Sino-Burmese border. Although this is of greatest concern to India, it fits a more general pattern of preparing a forward defense. In addition, China is modernizing its nuclear and missile arsenal despite the massive build-down by the United States and Russia.

Against this backdrop, Beijing's reluctance to pursue active diplomacy to resolve the Spratlys issue—even though its official position is that the resources should be jointly developed by the claimants—appears part of a strategy of maintaining ambiguity to maximize its freedom of action. The larger question of whether China will become fully integrated into international institutions and adopt international norms of behavior remains open and is the source of much uneasiness, particularly in Southeast Asia and Japan.

Japan's Role

Japan's emergence as a major economic power in the 1980s, its quest for a global political role commensurate with its economic and financial weight, and its tendencies to airbrush its history during the 1930s and 1940s, when combined with persistent tensions in U.S.-Japan relations are, in a nutshell, what lie behind concerns about Japan's intentions. Concern that an independent Japan may somehow harbor hegemonic ambitions in the Pacific continues to be part of the pathology of East Asia. This concern is most evident in China and Korea.

Inept Japanese diplomacy fuels such fears. In recent months, for example, two Japanese cabinet officials have resigned after making public comments questioning Japan's aggression in the Pacific during the 1930s and 1940s, further fueling doubts about Japan's future role in the region. Such behavior appears in the view of some Asian analysts to negate the bold efforts to exorcise the past made by former prime minister Morihiro Hosokawa, rendering his use of the term "aggression" and other acts of contrition more an expression of personal views than those of Japan as a whole.

Japan's Nuclear Program.   Such doubts about Japanese intentions have also been exacerbated by recent public statements by senior Japanese officials and disclosures in the Japanese press about official attitudes toward nuclear weapons. On August 1, 1994, *Mainichi Shimbun* reported that a top-secret Foreign Ministry report had stated that Japan should make sure it could acquire nuclear weapons if needed. "For the time being," said the report (the authenticity of which has not been questioned), "we will adopt a policy of not possessing nuclear arms.

But we will maintain the economic and technical potential of producing nuclear weapons."

Such views should not be surprising. Similar views have been publicly expressed before. A 1970 Defense White Paper (overseen by Yasuhiro Nakasone, then director of the Japanese Defense Agency), said that obtaining defensive nuclear weapons would not violate Japan's peace constitution. In July 1993, *Asahi Shimbun* reported that then Foreign Minister Kabun Muto, referring to the North Korean threat said, "If it comes down to the crunch, possessing the will that 'we can do it'—make nuclear weapons—is important."

Although Japan proclaims that nonproliferation is a key foreign policy priority, it has not (at least until very recently) even begun to view its continuing accumulation of plutonium as inconsistent with that goal. Japanese officials were stunned at the Asian reaction to its plutonium shipment from France to Japan in the fall of 1992.[8] Indeed, Japan has generally viewed its ambitious long-term nuclear energy program almost exclusively as an antidote to its own dearth of natural resources, as part of its traditional view of Japan as a small, resource-poor island. Japan has long had the capability to produce nuclear weapons. The combination of a post-World War II pacifist political culture (codified in Article Nine of its constitution and reinforced by the experience of being the only nation ever attacked with nuclear weapons) and the benefit of the U.S. nuclear umbrella has led Tokyo to eschew acquiring the bomb. Nonetheless, whatever its intentions, Japan is accumulating an ever-greater capability to produce a nuclear arsenal—along with a sophisticated delivery system, the H-2 rocket (at a cost of some $3 billion)—in short order.

However much Japan's quest for a closed fuel cycle may reflect hopes of energy independence, the public views expressed by senior members of Japan's nuclear establishment do little to reassure skeptics. Even as the IAEA was reporting 154 pounds of unaccounted-for plutonium in Japan's reprocessing plant at Tokai-Mura, leading experts such as Ryukichi Imai continued to argue, in the face of contrary evidence, that reactor-grade plutonium is not suited for weapons production. This has been authoritatively refuted by U.S. nuclear experts, including some with long experience manufacturing nuclear weapons, and by senior U.S. officials in discussions with the author.[9]

That leading members of Japan's science establishment seek to peddle such specious views only reinforces doubt about

Japan's intentions. Japan's technological prowess is closely watched by its neighbors. In addition to its supercomputer capabilities (useful in the design of nuclear weapons), Japan has acquired sophisticated laser enrichment for uranium. In February 1994, Tokyo successfully launched the H-2 rocket, which could provide not only long-range ballistic missile capability but also an independent reconnaissance capability (an initiative recommended by the recent Prime Minister's Review Commission).

Relations with China and Korea. Both the Sino-Japanese relationship (which is likely to become the most important bilateral link affecting stability in the Pacific in the twenty-first century) and Korean-Japanese relations continue to be haunted by suspicion and mistrust based on Japan's past behavior. One historic analogy that may prove a useful prism through which to view regional stability is a comparison of Sino-Japanese ties and the evolution of Franco-German relations.

For much of the century prior to World War II, Europe was unstable and engulfed in conflict because the two major powers, France and Germany, had adversarial relations. After World War II, they finally came to terms with each other, permitting the emergence of NATO and the evolution of the European Community. The analogous relationship in the Pacific, particularly over the coming two to three decades, is the Sino-Japanese relationship. Whether it moves from being a dependent variable (shaped by U.S.-Japan and U.S.-China relations) to an independent variable will be an important indicator of power realities in the Asia Pacific. Until that historic stage is reached, an underlying sense of -suspicion is likely to plague Japan's ties to China and similarly to Korea—particularly a post-reunification Korea.

The U.S. Role

One of the principal reasons why there is so much concern and uncertainty about the emergence of China and Japan is the *relative* decline of the United States in the region. This is true in both the military and economic spheres, even though in *absolute* terms, U.S. trade and investment in the Asia Pacific continue to grow significantly and U.S. military capabilities remain substantially greater than those of any other Pacific power. The net effect of these trends is likely to be a process that transforms the United States, over time, from the predominant power to a major power in the region.

In fact, the explosion of intra-Asian trade and investment in recent years has already begun to overshadow the trade and investment of the United States in much of the region. In military terms, the combined forces of nature and the Philippines Senate resulted in a U.S. decision to leave its bases in the Philippines in 1991. In the short term, although the resultant access strategy ("places, not bases") has sustained the U.S. bilateral alliance network, Asian perceptions in regard to the longer term are less certain. U.S. access to Singapore, use of ship repair facilities in Malaysia and perhaps in Indonesia, as well as enhanced bilateral military cooperation with all the ASEAN nations have underscored the continued U.S. security commitment. But longer-term Asian concerns are palpable. Indeed, rising interest in security dialogues and new multilateral mechanisms is a consequence of the regional perception of the need for a hedge against a (gradually) diminishing U.S. security presence in the region.

The Clinton administration's policies toward East Asia have added to Asian misgivings. After an auspicious beginning with the 1993 Tokyo meeting of the Group of Seven industrialized countries (G-7) and the APEC summit in Seattle, the promising renewed U.S. engagement in the Asia Pacific began to unravel, precisely (as a leaked memo from Assistant Secretary of State Winston Lord explained) because Asians "are beginning to resist the nature of that engagement."[10] Over the course of its first 15 months in office, the administration found itself in unusually public economic and/or political disputes with China (most-favored-nation rights [MFN], human rights, proliferation), Japan (trade), North Korea (proliferation), Singapore (caning of a U.S. citizen), Indonesia (trade and East Timor), Thailand (proliferation), Burma (political legitimacy), and more generally over differing approaches to human rights, labor rights, and the environment.

Lord's memo warned of an emerging malaise in U.S. relations with East Asia. The regional perception was that U.S. policy was both a heavy-handed unilateralism—Lord suggested that the United States is viewed as "an international nanny if not bully"—and, like much Clinton foreign policy, driven by narrow domestic special interests. In any case, when the United States was not torn between its commercial interests and promoting its values, it was baldly in search of markets, viewing Asia as a "jobs issue" and threatening unilateral action if markets were not opened. Although Clinton's reversal on MFN and a scaling down of trade expectations with Japan have alleviated some

Asian concern, serious questions about what sort of "New Pacific Community" the United States has in mind and doubts about United States reliability have not evaporated. This is likely to be evidenced in the November 1995 APEC meeting in Tokyo, where the declarations of intent to form a free-trade zone by 2020 will bog down in debates over Malaysia's East Asia Economic Caucus and differing interpretations of what APEC is or should become.

Asian Arms Race?

The amorphous fears about the United States, Japan, and China discussed above—and the fact that Japan has the third largest defense budget in the world ($42 billion), while China spends at least $22 billion (a lack of transparency leaves much to guesswork)[11]—help explain a sustained military buildup in the region that some have characterized as an arms race. Certainly some of the military procurement under way for the past decade is divorced from any impending threats, and there is no arms race in the sense of a cycle of action-reaction. But there are growing expenditures, which by 1995 may amount to more than $130 billion for East Asia.

Apart from a hedging against uncertainty, this phenomenon is explained by several factors. There are supply-side pressures from the end of the cold war, with arms industries in the United States, Europe, and Russia, in some desperation, creating an appealing buyers' market. At the same time, the region features the world's most dynamic economies with some new found wealth and, in many cases, military establishments with substantial political influence. However, in no country in East Asia is military spending increasing as a percentage of gross national product (GNP). Indeed, in this sense, it is declining. In addition, the Law of the Sea Treaty gave countries 200-mile EEZs. This helps explain why many, particularly ASEAN countries, have been acquiring air and sea capabilities over the past decade.

The regional security environment in Northeast Asia offers Japan as compelling a rationale for rethinking its plutonium policies as do the economics of the fuel cycle. Viewed from Tokyo, Northeast Asia is highly volatile. Against a background of a century of animosity, Japan faces a Russia likely to evolve in a nationalist direction even as it consolidates democracy and privatizes its economy. Continued uncertainty about post-Deng directions for China in the face of China's growing nuclear and missile program also raise the possibility of Sino-Japanese military competition. Not only is China rapidly modernizing its military, but it is leapfrogging a generation in missile and nuclear technology through technology acquisition and scientific help from Russia.

A lack of transparency leaves some doubt about the precise numbers, but the consensus view of U.S. analysts is that the Chinese triad (long-range and medium-range missiles, bombers, and sea-based delivery systems) totals between 200 and 300 weapons (including fission weapons with yields of 20 to 40 tons and thermonuclear weapons with 1 to 5 megaton yields). China has several dozen intercontinental ballistic missiles and roughly 100 intermediate-range ballistic missiles.[12] Two Chinese nuclear tests in the past year indicate that Beijing is modernizing its nuclear arsenal, perhaps MIRVing it in the process.

Moreover, China's nuclear calculus is global in nature. Given that it is one of the five declared nuclear powers, and potentially has India as well as Russia as a security concern, China's nuclear program can only be addressed in a global context, most probably in nuclear reduction talks among the five at some stage after the second Strategic Arms Reduction Treaty is implemented. Projecting out over the next quarter-century, there is clearly potential for Sino-Japanese nuclear (or opaque nuclear in Japan's case) competition.

In sum, China's quest for modernized force projection capabilities, Japan's impressive acquisition of dual-use capabilities, the dangers of nuclear and missile proliferation by North Korea, and ASEAN procurement patterns give cause for concern. This underscores the need for transparency and more discussion of threats, doctrine, and broad security concerns in the region, particularly because, apart from the Korean peninsula, no nation in the region views any other nation overtly as an adversary.

Nontraditional Security Threats

Beyond the previously noted historic concerns lie a host of nontraditional security concerns of increasing importance to the overall sense of well-being among the nations of the region. These include piracy, the environment, refugee flows, and illicit narcotics.

Piracy may be the closest to traditional concerns about the safety of the sea lanes—and also one of the most pressing. According to the Malaysian-based International Maritime

Bureau, from 1991 to 1993 incidents of piracy in the South and East China Seas accounted for half the total of such acts world-wide.[13] A large portion of this piracy has been staged by Chinese military forces. This has raised questions about whether these incidents have constituted action by enterprising local units or assertions of extraterritorial sovereignty.   In any case, it points to a need for new forms of cooperation on maritime surveillance and control of the sea lanes.

Refugee flows and narcotics trafficking are both issues that have a global, as well as a regional, dimension in terms of their management. Parallel concerns of a broad range of governments suggest possibilities for new cooperative endeavors. Environmental problems are of varied character. Issues such as global warming and the "greenhouse effect" are largely global in scope but have a regional dimension, for example, in managing rain forests. Some environmental issues may be subregional in scope, however. Acid rain from China, which has begun to appear in Japan, Korea, and parts of the Russian Far East, suggest a problem that may fit on a Northeast Asian agenda. Also of growing concern in the region is the depletion of fish resources, an issue that clearly lends itself to regional or subregional management.

Other Regional Concerns

Although the focus of this chapter has been on security threats, it is important to stress that virtually all nations in the region overwhelmingly emphasize the priority they all accord to economic growth. Moreover, there are two important, unprecedented trends: the degree and character of burgeoning economic interdependence—both transpacific and intra-Asian—and democratization. Although it is impossible to quantify the importance of either of these trends, both are increasingly critical determinants of international behavior.

Economic Growth

To put the regional economy in perspective, in 1960 the East Asian economies comprised 4 percent of world GNP. By 1990, they comprised some 25 percent of world GNP (roughly equal to that of the United States). By the year 2000, they are projected to account for one-third of world GNP.[14] Already, the seven leading East Asian economies have more than 40 percent of global bank reserves, up from 17 percent in 1980. The average savings rate of Asian economies is some 30 percent, compared to 8 percent for the G-7 economies. According to World Bank estimates, Asia will account for one-half of global GNP growth and one-half of global trade growth in the decade from 1990 to 2000, growing perhaps twice as fast as the United States and three times faster than Europe.

For the United States, whose two-way trade across the Pacific in 1993 reached $361 billion—some 50 percent more than its transatlantic trade—Asia is of critical importance. Equally impressive is the sustained growth of U.S.-Asia trade: from 1978 to 1991, U.S. transpacific trade *quadrupled* from $80 billion to $316 billion.[15] The diversity of East Asia's trade underscores the region's growing global economic importance. For example, in 1992 the European Union's trade with the Pacific Rim economies totalled $249 billion, surpassing its $206 billion trade across the Atlantic with the United States.[16]

Intra-Asian Patterns.　Perhaps the most remarkable aspect of Asia Pacific economic dynamism is the exponential advance of the "horizontal" integration of an intra-Asian trade and investment network, particularly over the past 10 to 15 years. As each East Asian economy has moved up the ladder of development, it has tended to accelerate the growth of those at the next tier of development. This pattern is evident in trade and investment figures. Intra-Asian trade now accounts for about 45 percent of total East Asia trade. When East Asian trade across the Pacific is added in, it amounts to almost two-thirds of total transpacific trade.[17] Taiwan is now the largest foreign investor in Malaysia and Vietnam. The other Asian newly industrializing economies are major investors in ASEAN economies. Hong Kong and Taiwan also account for more than two-thirds of foreign direct investment in China.

Ramifications.　To date, intra-Asian and transpacific economic interaction have created a synergy that is essential to sustaining economic growth, while the Asia Pacific has become an engine of global growth and enlarged common interests. But what are the political and/or strategic ramifications of this economic colossus for bilateral and multilateral relations in the region? And how does it affect the broader international behavior of Asia Pacific actors? One can only speculate what the impact on regional security perceptions would be if the region was suddenly plagued by several years of negative growth.

In the near term, the character of the U.S.-Japan, U.S-China, and Sino-Japanese relationships would be critical determinants of the political realities of the Asia Pacific. Over the longer term, Sino-Japanese relations will grow as a major factor in East Asian stability or the lack of it. In the interim, Sino-Japanese relations remain a dependent variable, with the United States the wild-card in the region.

Democratization

Ironically, the goals of enhancing human rights and democracy, which the United States is seeking to put on fast-forward, are unfolding in any case—albeit at an Asian rhythm and in an Asian style—propelled by the social and economic consequences of the failure of other political systems and the Asia Pacific's economic dynamism. A consistent pattern has emerged in East Asia over the past decade: when economic development has reached a stage where it has produced a large, urbanized middle class, these new social forces press for more accountability and political pluralism. This pattern is not unique to Asia, but it has been a consistent feature of the recent East Asian experience.

In the Philippines in 1986, the "people power" movement ousted Ferdinand Marcos. The success of that movement inspired South Korea and facilitated its transition to democracy in 1988. The demise of the Soviet Union helped Mongolia begin a democratic transition. Similarly Taiwan has made the transition from an authoritarian, Confucian-Leninist system to an essentially democratic system. In Bangkok, demonstrators armed with cellular phones pushed the Thai generals back into the barracks and solidified Thai democracy. One could also add Cambodia, where one result of the tortuous peace process has been democratic elections and a new democratically elected regime. It could also be argued that the Tiananmen incident occurred in part because China's economic reforms produced new social forces that its anachronistic political system could not accommodate.

Conclusion

One can only speculate about the impact of both economic considerations and more accountable governments on security questions. Certainly in South Asia, if either New Delhi or Islamabad were to follow populist aspirations, the results would not be an eclipse of conflict. It is a fair question as to whether even a democratic China would be an assertively nationalist nation. It remains to be seen whether these nascent East Asian realities are indeed creating a new calculus and fostering perceptions of a new set of interests and priorities that may redefine—if not reinvent—conceptions of security.

A more democratic Asia might, however, alleviate suspicions about the hidden intentions. Such suspicions usually lie behind most fears of insecurity. Their elimination would tend to temper ambitions, expand the prospects for cooperation, and minimize the prospects of conflict. By definition, any real Pacific Community requires shared interests, shared responsibility, and mutual respect. It will also increasingly require shared leadership. The difficulties experienced in the creation of APEC suggest that it will be, at best, a very protracted process before the Asia Pacific finds organizational expression for the notion of a security community in the Pacific. The danger lies in the interim, as traditional territorial disputes, historic rivalries, and suspicions fester among increasingly prosperous Asian nations with increasingly capable military assets.

Notes

1. See U.S. Department of Defense, *East Asia Strategy Initiative* (Washington, D.C.: Department of Defense, May 1991) for an official view of the U.S. role.

2. U.S. and Korean military analysts in discussions with the author.

3. See *New York Times*, July 21, 1994. China and Vietnam have respectively granted concessions to different U.S. companies in areas of overlapping claims in the Spratlys in a war of nerves.

4. See the article by Dr. Koo Chen-fu, chairman, Straits Exchange Foundation, entitled "Outlook for Cross-Strait Relations," in *PacNet*, no. 8 (Pacific Forum CSIS, Honolulu), March 1994.

5. Philip Shenon, "China Reaches Breakthrough with Taiwan," *New York Times*, August 8, 1994.

6. It must be stressed that these projections are worst-case scenarios that are not highly likely but not inconceivable.

7. See Jim Mann, *Los Angeles Times*, June 29, 1994, for documentation on Chinese pressure on North Korea prior to the visit of former U.S. president Jimmy Carter to North Korea. The author has also confirmed the Chinese role in influencing Pyongyang in discussions with U.S. officials.

8. Senior Foreign Ministry officials in discussions with the author.

9. National Academy of Sciences, *Management and Disposition of Excess Weapons Plutonium*, report of the Committee on International Security

and Arms Control (Washington, D.C.: National Academy Press, 1994). See also the view of former U.S. nuclear weapons designer J. Carson Mark, "Explosive Properties of Reactor-grade Plutonium," *Science & Global Security* 4 (1993).

10. "U.S. Aide Sees Relations with Asia in Peril," *Washington Post*, May 5, 1994.

11. See Desmond Ball, "Arms and Affluence," *International Security* 18 (winter 1993/94), for the most thorough analysis of Asian military spending and underlying rationales.

12. Data from Robert G. Sutter, "Chinese Nuclear Weapons and Arms Control Policies" (Congressional Research Service, Washington, D.C., March 25, 1994).

13. "Gunboat Diplomacy," *Far Eastern Economic Review*, June 16, 1994.

14. See "Asia Survey," *The Economist*, October 30, 1993.

15. Until 1994, trade in services, where the United States is a world leader (and is running large surpluses), was not included in standard trade balance figures.

16. Roger Cohen, "Like U.S., Western Europe Steps up Its Trade with Asia," *New York Times*, November 24, 1993, p. A-17.

17. See the International Trade Commission's important study of intra-Asian trade, "East Asia: Regional Integration and Implications for the United States" (Washington, D.C., May 1993).

3

The Anatomy of Anxiety in the Emerging East Asia Security Order

Oh Kwan-chi

It is paradoxical that all of a sudden, Northeast Asian countries, and to a lesser degree Southeast Asian ones as well, find themselves confronted with a world totally different from that with which they were familiar. This strange new post-cold war world, in which anxiety rather than certainty and composure is the rule, is not what they expected when the cold war ended.

While the cold war was being waged there were no uncertainties about potential threats. The identity of both allies and adversaries, the high risk of escalation inherent in possible conflict, and the nature and intent of security arrangements were clear to all. The end of the East-West confrontation has fundamentally altered the security environment, however, and made existing security policies and strategies incongruent with reality. As Soviet expansionism—a single threat supported by military power—ceased to exist, a multitude of unexpected security problems previously suppressed or unknown began to emerge. Because the existing security configuration was not designed to address more complicated, ambiguous, and fluid security problems, it is no wonder that countries in the Asia Pacific region are perplexed by the changed security milieu. Asia is groping for a new security arrangement congruent with the new situation. This is particularly so in Northeast Asia, where an acute East-West confrontation originated with the outbreak of the Korean War and has been further entrenched by two regional powers, Japan and China, that have mutually incompatible ideologies and policy orientations and compete with each other for regional influence.

Because the reduction of the U.S. military posture in the region is perceived to create a power vacuum, these two regional powers are expected to play a greater regional role for different reasons. China, while proclaiming "five principles of a peaceful coexistence," is suspected of pursuing expansionism—sometimes overtly and, in other cases, covertly—by flexing its military muscle. Cherishing the same values as North Korea, China is determined to prop up the North Korean regime at the expense of the international community. China may also be attempting to exploit North Korea in pursuit of its own interests. Meanwhile, Japan does not seem to have settled upon its future regional role, as is succinctly demonstrated by its extensive debates on that role and its return to the status of a "normal state." The problem with Japan is that much yet remains for it to do to win its neighbors' confidence. Sooner or later, Japan has to formulate its long-term policy toward China as an integral element of its regional security arrangements. The uncertainty surrounding future relations between Japan and China remains a major source of concern.

Another distinct feature of East Asia is that it is riddled with territorial disputes between regional powers and smaller countries. What makes the region unstable is the fact that these territorial disputes could easily lead to enmity, if not open hostilities, under the changed security environment. The unsettled "Northern Territories" issue between Japan and Russia has effectively barred them not only from improving political relations but also from advancing economic cooperation. Thus, unless the issue is resolved to both nations' satisfaction, there is only a remote possibility that the two countries will cooperate in building confidence and peacefully resolving regional issues. The dispute on the Senkaku Islands between Japan and China is another potential source of regional instability. China seems to have decided not to escalate the issue, although it repeatedly claims its sovereignty over the islands. China's underlying calculation is quite simple: Why should it antagonize Japan when Japanese capital and technology are badly needed for its ambitious economic development? Besides, the much publicized disputes over the Spratly Islands and several other border disputes have dragged on for years, mainly along the Chinese border. Needless to say, these territorial and border disputes, unless peacefully resolved, can foment distrust and enmity, lead to open hostilities, and undermine the stability of the region.

Causes of Security Anxiety

If anxiety and uncertainty characterize East Asia in a post-cold war world, what are the causes? There are a multitude of variables or factors affecting anxiety and uncertainty, some originating from past historical interactions. At the risk of oversimplification, it can be argued that the following five variables or strategic developments are the primary causes: (1) a continuing drawdown of U.S. forces from the Asia Pacific region; (2) the advent of economic blocs, the North American Free Trade Agreement (NAFTA) in particular; (3) the rapid rise of China as a future superpower; (4) uncertainties and unpredictability regarding Japan's future identity as a potential superpower; and (5) North Korea's nuclear weapons development.[1]

U.S. Military Posture

Of the above five variables, no doubt the overriding one is the perception within the region of a continuing reduction of U.S. military strength. The perception that the United States will not indefinitely sustain its present level of political, economic, and security engagement in East Asia is a major source of anxiety, notwithstanding the U.S. government's repeated assurances of continued American engagement in Asia and the Pacific, substantiated by ample U.S. military presence.[2] The first-phase force drawdown from South Korea, Japan, and the Philippines between 1990 and 1992, as prescribed by the Nunn-Warner Act, was construed as the onset of U.S. military disengagement in the region, even though it was painstakingly explained on the grounds of the significantly increased ability of Asian friends and allies to contribute to their own defense.

There is no doubt that the United States planned meticulously and acted with prudence. In South Korea, for example, the United States planned to retain a ground and air presence to deter aggression from North Korea while U.S. forces shifted from a leading to a supporting role within the coalition. The United States made its position clear by proclaiming as an essential element of long-term U.S. strategy the transition of the Republic of Korea (ROK) to the leading role in its own defense. The United States also pledged to continue to assist the ROK military in force improvement. Coalition structures and capabilities will be adjusted to match the strategy through training, combined exercises (such as Team Spirit, among others), and U.S. provision of certain capabilities unaffordable and unattainable to the ROK over the short or mid-term (strategic and operational intelligence, strategic and tactical air power, naval support, and selected ground combat capabilities). The United States further added that a U.S. force presence would be envisioned as long as the Korean people and government wanted it and threats to peace and stability remained.[3]

In November 1991, the United States decided to postpone the planned phase two troop reductions in South Korea because of the danger and uncertainty posed by North Korea's nuclear weapons program. Had reductions been undertaken as planned, the U.S. combat posture in South Korea would be a composite force of one mechanized and one combat aviation brigade, and one Tactical Fighter Wing, roughly one-third of the strength present at the beginning of the force adjustment. It was a timely decision that undoubtedly demonstrated the credibility of the U.S. policy of engagement to countries in the region that had apprehensively been watching to determine if the United States would live up to its promises. This was particularly so because in July 1991 the U.S. Air Force abandoned Clark Air Base in the Philippines, a valuable regional logistics hub, which had suffered extensive damage from the eruption of Mt. Pinatubo.

Trust in U.S. commitments was soon undermined, however, by a sequence of occurrences. In late December 1991, right after the departure from Clark Air Base, the U.S.-Philippines negotiations on the possibility of an extended withdrawal agreement ended abruptly. The United States was told by the Philippine government to withdraw all its forces from Subic Naval Base and Cubi Point Naval Air Station by the end of 1992. Because of the indispensable geostrategic value of the Subic and Cubi Point facilities for U.S. naval operations in the Asia Pacific region, countries in East Asia took the untimely closure of the bases, even though apparently decided by the Philippines, as another U.S.-planned measure to disengage from, or to reduce its military profile in, the region. As regional doubts about the U.S. security engagement mounted, so did doubts about U.S. political will. Countries in the region appear to be frustrated by U.S. indecisiveness in dealing with Serbia: instead of taking a resolute step, the United States looked on with folded arms. As a result, how can this region be confident of the U.S. will to engage in regional affairs when American lives and resources are at risk?

Economic Blocs

The often-cited extraordinary economic dynamism of the region cannot be sustained without the huge absorption capability of the American market and an open global trading system led by the United States and upheld by the U.S. military presence.[4] The conclusion of NAFTA was apprehensively perceived by the region as a U.S. first step to forming a regional bloc to effectively cut off North America from competition from East Asian countries. Thus, the agreement bodes ill for the future economic growth of the region, given the reliance of many Asian economies on access to America's market.

The rather devastating impact of NAFTA was somewhat relieved by the Clinton administration's policy reorientation to concurrently pursue a "New Pacific Community," one that might be constructed around an organization devoted to regional economic and security concerns. A strong candidate for the organization appears to be the Asia Pacific Economic Cooperation (APEC) forum. But APEC, for the foreseeable future, is not expected to provide either collective security or an environment for significant economic cooperation.[5]

China

Everybody seems to feel optimistic about China's economic future. This optimism is not groundless, in light of China's remarkable past performance. Annual growth rates averaged over 10 percent in the 1980s, thereby doubling China's gross national product (GNP) during the first decade of reform. Furthermore, as the Chinese economy rapidly integrates into the world economy, the economic interdependency between open economies is also deepened. Yet, in spite of all this good news, the region cannot dispel the suspicion that an economically powerful, but politically authoritarian, China may not be at peace with its neighbors.[6]

Japan

As a power vacuum, genuine or imagined, develops concomitant with the U.S. adjustment of its military posture in the Asia Pacific region, questions rise both within and outside Japan. How will Japan react to the changed circumstances? Will it reorient its political, economic, and security roles? Will Japan continue to uphold the U.S.-Japan security treaty even if the Russian threat is diminished? Japan has encouraged regional security thinking and was a moving force behind the agreement reached at the Post-Ministerial Conference of the Association of Southeast Asian Nations (ASEAN) to begin dealing with regional security issues. Furthermore, it was Japan that painstakingly tried to persuade ASEAN to recognize that a U.S. military presence was vital to their security. But, what if the United

States has to reduce its military profile in the region because of domestic politics? Will Japan take over the security role it has hitherto played? Thus, uncertainties and the unpredictability of the future identity of Japan give rise to anxiety.

North Korea

Every country in the Asia Pacific region fully understands the seriousness of North Korea's nuclear weapons development, which may trigger eventual nuclear proliferation in the region and fundamentally alter the regional security equation. The dilemma is that the region lacks effective measures to induce or oblige North Korea to relinquish its nuclear weapons program. Thus, even if a regional approach for dealing with North Korea's fixation on nuclear weapons seems to be desirable, no corporate movement has taken place.

China was expected to play a key role in dissuading North Korea from holding fast to its nuclear weapons development program, but it has disappointed the concerned parties by not exercising economic and political leverage. China appears to be erroneously calculating that the benefits of sustaining a pliable North Korean regime outweigh the expected cost of a nuclear-ized North Korea. Furthermore, by assuming an equivocal attitude on the issues, China is suspected of skillfully taking advantage of the North Korean nuclear problem in negotiating with the United States, Japan, and South Korea. China's frequent abstention from voting on the North Korean nuclear issue at the United Nations (UN) and the International Atomic Energy Agency (IAEA) seems to clearly underscore this point.

On October 21, 1994, after many complications, the United States and North Korea concluded an "Agreed Framework" accord on overall resolution of the nuclear issue on the Korean peninsula. Besides setting a bad precedent by rewarding a nation for violating international laws, the accord exempts North Korea from some of its obligations under the IAEA safeguards agreement (i.e., challenge inspection of suspected facilities) for at least another five years. This signifies that North Korea will not only be immune from charges of past noncompliance with, and possible violation of, the safeguards agreement (by extraction of weapon-grade plutonium), but will also be given another five years to hold the plutonium or to perfect a nuclear weapon. Notwithstanding conclusion of the accord between the United States and North Korea, therefore, we have to wait at least another five years to see whether the nuclear issue will be completely resolved. Furthermore, in light of North Korea's past record of noncompliance, it is open to doubt whether North Korea will faithfully live up to the Geneva accord.

Security Concerns

The five primary variables discussed above seem to generate anxiety in East Asia. Such anxiety also takes on more definite forms: misgivings about possible new conflict on the Korean peninsula; the threat of nuclear proliferation; apprehensions about any emerging regional security order; the insecurity of the regional economic and trading system; and uneasiness over emerging nontraditional security issues.

Potential for Conflict on the Korean Peninsula

Renewed hostilities on the Korean peninsula would completely disrupt the fragile regional order and deprive the region of any chance to deliberate on confidence and security building arrangements. No one in the region would benefit by a new conflict except North Korea, the only potential provoker. China will suffer most because its whole modernization program is at stake. Open hostilities on the Korean peninsula will certainly make the Chinese business environment less favorable to foreigners and will disproportionately increase the risk of their investments in China. Because China is the only remaining ally of North Korea, it could be forced to get involved in the war. If China supports North Korea, either by taking political measures in the international arena or by supplying war material or sending an army of volunteers, it will necessarily incur an array of economic sanctions. As a consequence, foreigners doing business with China will withdraw their investment. Needless to say, China's ambitious economic development programs entirely hinge upon foreign investment and international trade.

Because the Chinese Communist regime can continue to claim legitimacy in this age of market democracy only by rapid improvement of the standard of living of its people, China may have a strong disincentive to get involved in a war provoked by North Korea. If China, to minimize the damage to its economy caused by conflict, restrains itself from taking sides with North Korea, then relations between the two will turn sour and could eventually be broken. This is not what China wants either. In the already dwindled socialist camp, China badly needs solidarity with the remaining Communist countries in order to legitimize communism as an official ideology.

Furthermore, a rogue North Korea could be a valuable asset, exploitable to enhance China's diplomatic leverage, as long as China can exercise influence over it. All these considerations amount to a Chinese dilemma in case of renewed conflict on the Korean peninsula. All other countries in the region will also suffer a loss, large or small, from a renewed war, especially the ROK and the United States. Peace and stability on the Korean peninsula therefore benefit every country in the region.

Nevertheless, danger of a renewed war on the Korean peninsula provoked by North Korea remains. Chances of open hostilities could increase if the North Korean regime believes that unification on its own terms (by force) could provide a more favorable and feasible way out of the multitude of crises it now faces. All evidence indicates that North Korea is beleaguered by manifold ideological, economic, and diplomatic crises as well as more fundamental crises of identity and legitimacy.

In the process of political development, an identity crisis occurs when a nation finds that what it had once unquestioningly accepted as the physical and psychological definitions of its collective self are no longer acceptable under new historic conditions.[7] This is the case for North Korea. After World War II, the Soviet military government completely rooted out the prevailing social institutions of a traditional society thousands of years old and replaced then with socialist ones quite alien to the people. The people then underwent an unprecedented social mobilization and were driven to a fratricidal war by Kim Il Sung, a Soviet protégé installed at the head of the North Korean regime by the Kremlin.

North Korea's identity problem could only be suppressed by its intensive programs of political socialization, which could not be sustained if the regime's capacity for social control deteriorated. This occurred when Communist regimes in Eastern Europe and the Soviet Union collapsed. Confronted with the same danger, North Korea launched an extensive propaganda offensive to persuade its people to safeguard its socialist system. This implies that North Korea perceived itself to be in an identity as well an ideological crisis, one that could trigger revolutionary transformation of the society.

The North Korean regime claims that the legitimacy of its political power is derived from democratic political processes. This is a pure falsehood. Contrary to its claim, the regime tried to legitimize its power by citing Kim Il Sung's stupendous service to the Korean people through his armed struggle against imperialist Japan to win Korea's independence; the great achievements of the regime under Kim's guidance since 1945; and the indispensability of Kim's leadership in building a Communist utopia. These three foundations were based on an extensively fabricated personality cult of Kim Il Sung. Consequently, they can hardly be maintained once the society is opened. While Kim Il Sung was alive, the North Korean regime tried to legitimize his son Kim Jong Il's succession to power by arguing that he was the only candidate who could ensure an undistorted continuity of the revolution to realize the Communist society started by his father. The regime accordingly launched a campaign to create a personality cult of Kim Jong Il concurrent with a gradual transfer of power and responsibility to him.

Nevertheless, the North Korean leadership does not seem confident that it can convince its people of the legitimacy of the power succession. Consequently, after the death of Kim Il Sung, the leadership borrowed the will of the deceased to further justify the junior Kim's succession to power. This signals that the legitimacy of Kim Jong Il's succession to power has to be derived from the deceased. The heir apparent, Kim Jong Il, is ultimately obliged to justify his power based on Kim Il Sung's legitimacy alone; thus the North Korean regime under Kim Jong Il is in a legitimacy crisis.

Evidence seems to indicate that North Korea is beleaguered with economic difficulties. For the past four consecutive years (1990 to 1993) the economy was estimated to record negative growth, averaging -5 percent per year. Many factors contributed to this poor performance: the unfavorable weather; the loss of sources of cheap energy and capital goods; dwindled foreign trade with Russia, other members of the Commonwealth of Independent States, East European countries, and, to a lesser degree, China; the inefficiency of its economic system; and excessive military expenditures that overtaxed the economy. Economic retrogression not only brought about an ever-falling standard of living, but also enlarged the feeling of relative deprivation, especially in view of South Korea's steadily improving material advantages. Because this is diametrically opposite to what was promised by the regime, North Korea's economic crises have strong political implications.

The end of an ideological confrontation, the subsequent spread of market democracy, and the pursuit of economic interests as an overriding trend worldwide have rapidly deprived

North Korea of its diplomatic base. It is not difficult to appreciate North Korea's diplomatic dilemma simply by noting that the demise of the Soviet Union means a complete loss of its ideological foundation; a benign ally; a source of capital, technologies, cheap energy, and modern weapons; the principal foreign market for its exports; and, above all, a model country to copy. North Korea used to maintain some influence over the Third World until the collapse of the former Soviet Union. It completely lost its credibility in the post-cold war era, in which economic rather than ideological interests are dominant. Even China, having established formal relations with the ROK, cannot be taken for granted; there is no assurance China will support North Korea without reservation on any issue. In brief, North Korea is encountering a diplomatic crisis.

The ultimate collapse of North Korea's social system is made more likely by its intrinsic contradictions. The most important are those between Kim Il Sung's totalistic utopian or eschatological visions and the poor performance of the regime; between the regime's participatory democratic and totalitarian components; between the high level of social mobilization effected by the regime and the attempts to totally control all the mobilized groups; between the better educated elites required by modernization and the attempts to control the flow of information; and between a shift in generations and the refusal to change.[8] Needless to say, these systemic contradictions have gradually alienated the people from the regime and created an atmosphere ruled by cynicism.

The synergy of the crises and the contradictions of the totalitarian dictatorship generate powerful social forces that may threaten the very survival of the regime. Kim Jong Il may still feel confident that threatening forces will remain under control if the regime can keep the society from being opened to the outside world (and to South Korea in particular). He also appears to fully appreciate that, if the North Korean society is exposed to South Korea, the synergistic effects of crises and contradictions will be so explosive as to collapse the regime. An opened North Korean society will quickly and thoroughly be penetrated by South Korea, as West Germany penetrated East Germany, further deepening the manifold crises and making the contradictions even more acute.

As previously noted, the legitimacy of the North Korean regime relied solely on fabricated exploits, especially of Kim Il

Sung, said to have taken place during the independence movement of the 1930s and 1940s against imperialist Japan. Kim even
ridiculed the ROK by claiming that he returned to Korea in 1945
triumphantly waging a joint operation of his revolutionary
army with the Soviet forces to defeat the fleeing Japanese imperialist army.[9] Throwing open the North Korean society to the outside world will certainly disclose the fabrication of Kim's
achievements, which will then lead to the disenchantment of the
whole population.

In light of the anticipated fatal blow to the regime that would
result from opening the system, policy options for the North
Korean regime are quite limited. The regime cannot adopt a full-
fledged open door policy unless it is forced to risk unacceptable
social transformation. Even the Chinese model of economic
development can hardly be a pattern because it will certainly lift
the lid on channels of external information. The regime is apprehensive of peaceful coexistence between South and North Korea;
witness its outright refusal of the family search campaign
encompassing the exchange of letters and visits among families
separated in the South and North. It should be stressed that
North Korea's phobia against opening its society is derived from
its cognizance that the synergistic effects of the regime's manifold crises and contradictions will be so explosive as to break
down the system. This would be particularly so because South
Korea—a nation of the same people, but under a different social
system—furnishes an authentic frame of reference and a source
of truth to the North Korean people, proving that they were
cheated by the regime, that they underwent undue and mean-
ingless hardships under the regime, that the regime is the very
source of inter-Korean animosity and an obstacle to peaceful and
democratic national reunification, and that Kim Il Sung was the
ringleader personally responsible for the tragedy of the fratricidal war of the 1950s.

No state can completely control the flow of information.
There is no exception, even in the case of North Korea. Korean-
Chinese visitors from neighboring China carry information
about South Korea to their relatives in North Korea. Information
about South Korea also flows in through foreign visitors, travel
abroad, students returning from studying abroad, foreign
envoys, North Korean visitors to the South, and various publications, among others. Thus, it is just a matter of time before North
Korea is penetrated by the South, the consequences of which the

North Korean leaders must clearly perceive. In this regard, the North's regime is haunted by the thought that a threat of absorption into the South is real and ever-mounting and that it needs to take decisive action to reverse the tide.[10] The logical conclusion is, of course, to root out the very source of the threat. This is the way in which the North Korean regime views the matter of national reunification. It is not so much desirable as it is a matter of life and death for them. This is why a structural instability exists on the Korean peninsula and why concerns about a renewed conflict remain.

Nuclear Proliferation

North Korea's suspect nuclear weapons development program constitutes the core of the nuclear proliferation issue in the Asia Pacific region. According to a former high-ranking North Korean diplomat who defected to South Korea in 1991, there is consensus among North Korean diplomats that "no country will rally or insult or threaten North Korea once it possesses nuclear weapons."[11] Although the statement apparently connotes a defensive purpose for North Korea's nuclear program, it should not be literally interpreted. A more precise interpretation is as follows: whatever North Korea may do, no country will hold it in check once it possesses nuclear weapons.

Then, what would North Korea like to do? The answer has already been presented in the previous section. If we accept the proposition that the very existence of South Korea in the southern part of the peninsula is perceived by the North Korean regime as posing an ever-mounting threat to its survival, then the apparently irrational behavior of the regime can be construed as perfectly rational. Thus, the development of nuclear weapons should be recognized as a logical consequence of the regime's threat perception. We should not, however, jump to the conclusion that North Korea's regime can be dissuaded from developing nuclear weapons by alleviating its threat perception or by guaranteeing its security, as advocated by so many scholars and policymakers.[12] Succinctly expounded, the perceived threat is not a military one; hence, there is little room for any outsiders to help as long as the North sticks to its own way.

To cope with the perceived threat, the North Korean regime has concentrated its energies on how to unify the peninsula on its own terms. The North, in order to attain unification, has mapped out two strategies: the so-called "liberation war" and subversion, the latter being supplementary in nature. It is no secret that North Korea has built up its armed forces to attempt another surprise attack on South Korea. The North Korean military edge over the South is so great that North Korean leaders must feel quite confident of a military victory. With a lightning strike they could realize their long-cherished dream of a communized peninsula if they could somehow block U.S. intervention in the war.

The North Korean leaders calculate that, to ensure U.S. non-intervention, they need to foster circumstances under which the United States is obliged to withdraw its forces from the South and be further restrained from intervening in Korean affairs. This is why we witnessed North Korea for decades making persistent demands for a peace treaty between it and the United States and a nonaggression pact between the South and the North.[13] Once the treaties are concluded, the North calculates that it can stir up public opinion in the United States to demand withdrawal of U.S forces from the peninsula. Why should U.S. forces continue to be stationed on the peninsula when peace is firmly secured by the two Koreas?

From the viewpoint of the North Korean leadership, the once much acclaimed inter-Korean accord, "Agreement on Reconciliation, Nonaggression, and Exchanges and Cooperation," concluded on December 13, 1991, is nothing but a nonaggression pact. From the very beginning the North insisted on adoption of a joint declaration on nonaggression rather than a comprehensive accord dealing with multifaceted exchanges and cooperation. North Korea, however, gave an unwilling consent to the inter-Korean agreement because it thought it could still achieve its long-standing goal by intentionally making all the other clauses except the clause on nonaggression a dead letter. This could easily be done by employing stalling tactics in negotiations on how to implement exchanges and cooperation in humanitarian, economic, cultural, and diplomatic fields, while a propaganda offensive was being launched to enforce the nonaggression clause.

Having achieved its first objective, North Korea will no doubt press for attainment of the second objective of its grand design, a peace treaty with the United States. We have already witnessed North Korea's demand for the peace treaty at the Geneva meeting and its request for withdrawal of Chinese delegates to the Military Armistice Commission—which stopped functioning due to North Korea's failure to attend—in addition to the well-known pressure on the Neutral Nations Supervisory Commission to withdraw.

While promoting a peace offensive, the North Korean regime must have searched for an alternative means to win the conceived liberation war and arrived at the nuclear option. Nuclear weapons can, the North realizes, be employed for multifaceted uses. Some of the more important ones, depending on the circumstances, include the following:

- The possession of tactical nuclear weapons, with their potential for swiftly incapacitating defensive forces, would provide the means to launch a successful all-out surprise attack on the South. (The North's development and stockpiling of chemical and biological weapons prove how eager it is to achieve just such a capability.)

- Nuclear weapons would neutralize the threat of U.S. nuclear retaliation when the North invades the South.

- If a conventional attack on the South were to fail and a massive retaliation including the expansion of such a war into the North by the ROK-U.S. Combined Forces was imminent, nuclear weapons might successfully deter such retaliation by threatening a nuclear attack on Seoul or the Combined Forces.

- Nuclear weapons would provide very effective political leverage. To obtain political or economic concessions from the South, or to press for compliance with its demands, the North Korean regime would never cease using nuclear blackmail. This would certainly extend to the international arena.

- North Korea may threaten to target U.S. forces in the event of renewed conflict on the Korean peninsula. This would certainly influence public opinion in America and possibly create political pressure for a massive reduction of U.S. forces in Korea. From an operational viewpoint, the threat of use of nuclear weapons on U.S. forces would render wartime deployment of the forces extremely complicated.

Thus, the North Korean regime might be convinced that nuclear weapons would enable it to successfully launch an all-out surprise attack on the South and that any counterattack by ROK-U.S. Combined Forces could be deterred.[14] The implication of this is straightforward: North Korea's possession of nuclear weapons will make the North's military provocations much easier and safer. Therefore, the military tension and risk of war on the peninsula would be greatly heightened by North Korean development of nuclear weapons.

It is not expected that North Korea's nuclear development would, at least in the short term, trigger a chain reaction of nuclear proliferation in Northeast Asia. Neither Japan nor South Korea is expected to launch a nuclear weapons program to cope with the North Korean nuclear threat, even that threat increases by a quantum leap. Once the North completes its Rodong missiles armed with nuclear warheads, Japan will be immediately threatened. Japan will be subjected to North Korean nuclear blackmail in connection with negotiations on diplomatic relations, attempts to control illegal monetary remittances to the North, and its active participation in UN sanctions on North Korea, if imposed. Furthermore, North Korea may threaten to target U.S. military bases in Japan in the event of an all-out war. The threat will materialize if the North miscalculates that such a nuclear attack will successfully eliminate the threat of U.S. military intervention in the conflict on the Korean peninsula, or if the North is driven to despair by a complete defeat in the war.

If the North Korean nuclear threat is to be seriously considered, Japan will face a dilemma. Should it develop a military capability to launch a preemptive strike on North Korean high-value targets? Should a demand be made for the withdrawal of U.S. forces in Japan and a ban placed on the use of ports by U.S. naval forces? Or, should Japan resort to U.S. retaliatory forces augmented by a theater missile defense system as discussed with the United States? The first alternative will certainly arouse the region's misgivings about Japanese militarism and may even trigger an unprecedented arms race among regional powers and lesser ones as well. The second alternative will tear the U.S.-Japan alliance apart and fundamentally change the regional security equation.

Should Japan opt for the second alternative, Japanese public opinion will change to demand a military buildup and, sooner or later, a militarily strong Japan will emerge. Furthermore, the United States will be obliged to restructure its military roles and deployment in the Asia Pacific region, possibly toward an accelerated reduction in view of the loss of Japanese burden sharing and difficulty in acquiring new bases elsewhere. Thus, opting for either of the first two alternatives will drastically increase regional instability. At this moment it is more likely that Japan will continue to rely on U.S. retaliatory capabilities to deter any future North Korean nuclear attacks. Whatever course of action Japan may take, there is no question about the destabilizing impact of North Korean nuclear developments on Japan and the region.

Emerging Regional Security Order

When a region is in a transitional period of total change, nothing can be certain and concrete with regard to a final state. East Asia cannot be an exception to the rule and the extent of uncertainty and unpredictability concerning its future security order seems to far exceed that of any other region experiencing a similar transformation at the end of the East-West confrontation. Geographical vastness, cultural plurality, and uneven economic development may contribute to this unique feature, but the more fundamental variables that shape it are contending values among the four major players; the perception that the United States is in decline and disengaging from East Asia; the relative rise of Japan and China, with ambiguity regarding their strategic concepts; and the uncertainty of economic reform and political development in Russia.

Countries with mutually incompatible ideologies can live together as long as their political, economic, and security interactions are so limited that each can pursue its own policies without affecting the others. This, however, is not the case in East Asia. As China, holding fast to socialism, assumes an intransigent stance toward dissenters and shuns any political reforms, not infrequent ideological disputes with the democratic camp arise because of ever-deepening economic interdependence. The disputes over Chinese violations of human rights are nothing but a surrogate for the ideological dispute. We can hardly expect these disputes to foster an environment conducive to confidence and cooperative security building. If confidence cannot be built and mistrust prevails among major regional powers, no one can hope that a stable and peaceful regional security order will emerge as time passes. Thus, apprehensions about the future regional security order will linger as long as regional powers are divided into two opposing camps by mutually contending ideologies and values.

The U.S. Role.   The United States' desire to engage and
continue to play a leadership role in political, economic, and
military affairs in East Asia is accepted without any reservations
by most countries of the region (with the notable exception of
China). But when it comes to the calculus of costs and benefits,
no one seems convinced of the U.S. will to remain as a leading
security partner in East Asia and to sustain a military profile
commensurate with a leadership role. This is particularly so
in view of what the United States wants to be included in its
calculus.

To succeed as the leader in the security partnership, the
United States has to lower costs associated with its leadership
role while setting two conditions: first, its allies are required to
contribute to mutual security; second, its allies must be sensitive
to the linkages between a sustained U.S. commitment to their
security on the one hand and their actions in such areas as trade
policy, technology transfer, and participation in multinational
security operations on the other.[15] If any of these conditions are
not met by any ally or allies, overt or covert disputes will arise
with the United States. If the dispute is not resolved smoothly,
if public feeling that the allies took advantage of U.S. generosity
by pursuing their own narrow interests cannot be avoided,
then the U.S. government will not be able to sustain the military
posture required to play a security leadership role. Thus, with
the explicit conditions of sustaining U.S. security leadership
absent unquestioned U.S. generosity, countries in the region are
worried.

The misgivings are most complex when it comes to Japan.
According to Ezra Vogel, many Americans now feel that the Japanese took advantage of their generosity by pursuing their own
narrow interests. Even when the Japanese became rich, they did
not assume their fair share of the burdens of maintaining peace.
Instead, Japan unfairly protected its markets from foreign goods,
copied American technology, and engaged in predatory practices
to destroy American industry.[16] Suppose the U.S. government is
obliged to draw down U.S. forces in Japan under political pressure. Other countries, which have indirectly benefited from U.S.
forces in Japan, will also lose because the security services rendered by the U.S. forces are not divisible.

This is the well-known textbook case of product indivisibil-
ity in which the exclusion principle cannot be applied; other
countries in the region cannot be prevented from consuming the
security services rendered by U.S. forces simply because they do

not pay for them.[17] Thus, other countries are subsidized for their security by Japan, which pays for the stationing of U.S. forces. In this sense, they are free riders. By the same logic, Japan cannot be prevented from consuming security services rendered by U.S. forces in other countries even if Japan does not pay for them. As a consequence, the quantity of security services rendered by U.S. forces is less than it would be if Japan were charged for the services. Therefore, any disputes between the United States and Japan and a resultant reduction of U.S. military presence in Japan will adversely affect other smaller allies' security in East Asia.

The Role of the People's Republic of China (PRC).   The past decade's record of security consultations with China clearly demonstrated the limitations on how far major regional powers with contending ideologies and values can cooperate in security affairs. This is not surprising in view of Chinese political tradition and national strategy, in addition to the resurgence of conservatism after the Tiananmen Square massacre of 1989. According to Fu Zhengyuan, China is a society that can be characterized by the following dominant characteristics: concentration of power in the hands of a few elites without institutional checks; law as a tool to control the populace; omnipotent state power; and individuals as subject and property of the state.[18]

The Chinese autocracy always pursued a security policy of combining force and appeasement measures, a military strategy of allying with a distant country to conquer or subjugate a neighboring one, and a foreign policy of employing a less threatening barbarian to bridle a more threatening one. A stable and peaceful world based on shared values is totally incompatible with Chinese autocracy. Only coolheaded calculations of costs and benefits determine Chinese security policy.

China, apprehensive of a militarily strong Japan, recognizes some merit in a U.S.-Japanese alliance that can effectively hold a resurgence of Japanese militarism in check. On the other hand, the same U.S.-Japanese alliance will become a powerful prop and mainstay of East Asia, which can in turn contain possible Chinese expansionism and adventurism. Thus, in this post-cold war era it is the single objective of Chinese policy toward Japan that Japan remain an independent civilian power with an abrogated U.S.-Japanese security treaty, while expanding Chinese-Japanese economic cooperation. China's attitude toward the United States appears to be basically hostile. To China, the United States is the only power that has both the political will and the military capacity to circumscribe its exercise of hegemony and power projection. In addition, the United States demands of China protection of human rights, a cessation of oppression of ethnic minorities, and an opening of its markets for U.S. exports under the continued threat of economic sanctions.

Although uncertainties remain as to future Chinese security policy, depending on the direction of its domestic development, the region has noted many evil omens that forebode a more assertive and uncooperative China in coming decades: the ruthless use of force in 1974 in the Paracel operation to oust the South Vietnamese garrison force; the military occupation of six Spratly Islands after a naval engagement in 1988; unilateral promulgation of a statute declaring the Paracel and Spratly Islands integral parts of the mainland; the granting of an offshore oil concession to Crestone Energy Corporation of Colorado, thereby humiliating Vietnam; and the unusually rapid increase in the Chinese defense budget, which has doubled over the past five years. Thus, many students of current China do not hesitate to express their concern that an economically and militarily stronger China will be a regional power with wider global commitment but fewer responsibilities and less caution, and will contend for patrimonial hegemony in the region.[19]

Japan's Role. Japan seems to realize that it should prepare to bear its share of costs for maintaining a stable international economic and political order in a system of plural leadership by major economic powers because the United States is no longer willing and able to endure the burden.[20] Some tasks suggested for Japan in a system of plural leadership are a greater responsibility in international financial markets, promotion of economic and regional cooperation, an efficient allocation of its foreign aid, initiation of world environmental protection, and creation of a global partnership with the United States.[21]

Note that discussion of Japan's military role is totally missing here. Japan formulates its security policy as a comprehensive concept centered on the economic and political dimensions of national security. Furthermore, that policy is solely determined by domestic factors, such as the structure of the state (i.e., institutions ensuring civilian control over the military) and sociolegal norms (i.e., a strong aversion to militarism).[22] Consequently, Japan's contribution to regional and world security will have to be basically nonmilitary in the post-cold war era.[23]

Japan's thinking on security affairs invites many questions. What if the United States is forced by domestic political pressure to reduce its military posture in the Asia Pacific region regardless of uncertainties about the region's strategic milieu and apprehension over China's assertive foreign policy? Will a comprehensive security policy centered on economic and political dimensions without the military dimension guarantee Japan's security and regional stability? Can Japan justify the formulation of its security policy solely in the context of domestic factors without due regard to changes in the outside world? Thus, Japan's future security role in the region, despite Japan's seemingly novel concept of comprehensive security, is yet to be defined.

The Future of Russia.   Because of its sheer size, there is no question about the critical importance of Russia's future economic and political development to the security of East Asia. We cannot be certain of Russia's future, however, due to the political leadership's recurrent wavering in their resolution to push forward the economic reform that will without doubt determine the destiny of the nation. This is understandable in view of the grave risks posed by massive unemployment—somewhere between 12 and 20 million (more than one-fifth of Russia's work force) by the end of 1994—as inefficient factories are dismantled by cutting back or eliminating subsidies to industries.[24] The only way to avoid 20 percent unemployment is to create jobs by promoting private business while the government continues restructuring large state enterprises, reducing subsidies to inefficient industries to avoid layoffs, and applying strict bankruptcy law. But creating private enterprises to absorb the layoffs from large state enterprises takes time, while saving jobs at the latter by subsidies seems more tempting to the political leadership. There is also some reservation about calling Russia's political system democratic in the full sense of Western liberal democracy because too much power rests with the president, no new judiciary exists, and there is no real role for independent political organizations such as trade unions and political parties. Thus, with only partly institutionalized democracy, apprehension remains about the possibility of the resurgence of an authoritarian regime or of a Slavic nationalism that would have adverse repercussions on Russia's foreign policy and security role in East Asia.

The four variables just surveyed are likely to interact with one another to give rise to an amplified uncertainty and unpredictability regarding the future regional order in the Asia Pacific region. Because major regional powers are supposed to play a leading role in shaping the order, and the above-mentioned variables are closely associated with them, we can hardly expect that a stable and cooperative regional order will emerge in the coming decades. Rather, it will more likely be interspersed with recurring tensions caused by assertive Chinese foreign and military policies and the region's enervation and appeasement toward China.

Insecurity of the Regional Economic System

Were it not for a stable international economic and trading system upheld by U.S. military presence and huge American markets for the regions' exports, the highly praised dynamic economic growth of East Asia would not have been possible. This will also be true in the coming decades, given the rather limited absorption capacity of other current and future super-economies, including Japan and China. Hence, it is quite natural that countries in East Asia have misgivings about U.S.-Japan trade disputes that might eventually trigger an ever-escalating economic war or arouse American emotionalism due to growing doubts about the ability of U.S. corporations to compete against Japanese firms, to provide jobs, and to offer a promising economic future for the next generation of Americans.[25] Either case will be followed by political pressure to reduce the U.S. military profile in the region and to form a regional bloc to effectively cut off foreign competition.[26] Initial Asian concerns over NAFTA can be construed in this context. Thus, a trade dispute between the United States and Japan could lead to a loss of American markets for regional exports that, in turn, would deprive the region of any opportunity for future economic prosperity.

It is noteworthy that the United States records a trade deficit not only with Japan but also with the East Asian newly industrialized economies (NIEs). This signifies that NIEs produce goods on capital and technologies borrowed from Japan and then export them to U.S. markets to pay for imports from Japan and for external debts as well. Thus, Japan contributes to the U.S. trade deficit not only through bilateral trade, but also through more indirect trilateral trade. In 1992, for example, the United States had a trade deficit of $52.6 billion with Japan and a $28.9 billion deficit with East Asian NIEs, while the NIEs had a trade deficit of $10.8 billion with Japan. It is quite understandable how seriously countries in the region are following the U.S.-Japan trade talks that, depending on their final outcome, will decisively affect their economic security in the coming decades.

Nontraditional Security Issues

With the diminished conventional military threat in East Asia, nontraditional security issues are gaining weight and need to be addressed properly. Some of the more important issues are territorial disputes, security of the sea lanes, drug trafficking, environmental degradation, and disputes concerning development of oceanic and seabed resources.

Territorial Disputes.   At issue in territorial and boundary disputes are fish resources and oil and gas believed to lie beneath the region's many islands, particularly in the region around the islands in the East and South China Seas. Of the 15 maritime borders in the South China Sea, 12 are in dispute, with most involving China.[27] China has declared the Senkaku, the Paracel, and the Spratly Islands, the associated surrounding waters, and the subsea shelf inalienable parts of the People's Republic. The reason why China is so assertive toward these islands is quite simple: the surrounding waters are estimated to hold oil reserves of up to 100 billion barrels for which only the Southeast Asian countries contend with China.[28]

China, in the face of protests from Japan and Southeast Asia, has taken a seemingly conciliatory posture by stating that it will resolve the disputes peacefully, and by making overtures to the countries concerned for joint development of oceanic and seabed resources.[29] Southeast Asians are, however, suspicious of China's suggestion. China may manipulate any agreements on joint development so as to oblige the signatories to acquiesce in Chinese claims of sovereignty over the disputed territories.

The strategic implications of China's formal claims in these waters should also not be overlooked. China, having laid the legal foundation to protect its claimed territories and resources within a 200-mile Exclusive Economic Zone, can control the sea lanes vital to East Asia. In fact, the disputed Chinese territorial waters statute explicitly stipulates China's right to use military force to prevent unauthorized foreign ships from entering its "territorial waters" surrounding the islands in the East and South China Seas. If executed, this means virtually no foreign ships or aircraft can enter this region, which has hitherto been international waters, without China's authorization.

Sea Lane Security. The frequent piracy committed by the Chinese navy in the South China Sea is also not irrelevant to the territorial disputes. Of a total of 98 piracy incidents in the 18 months after the middle of 1992, China was involved in 30.[30] The number of incidents increased after the Chinese government issued special orders to the Chinese navy, the National Maritime Police, and the customs authorities to stamp out the smuggling of goods into China. Because the government's measures to firm up control of smuggling include a prize for uncovering contraband, the navy and others are so zealous that they fail to respect freedom of navigation on the open seas. The Chinese government pretends not to be aware of the piracy because these outlaws enforce the government's claimed sovereignty over the seas. Thus, China's moves with respect to the Spratly Islands have succinctly disclosed its strategic intentions as it grows stronger militarily on the basis of rapid economic growth.[31]

Drug Trafficking. Southeast Asia continues to remain a major producer of illicit opium despite the initiatives of the governments concerned to eradicate illicit opium poppy cultivation.[32] Illicit heroin laboratories also continue to operate in the Golden Triangle of Southeast Asia. Furthermore, China, Hong Kong, Japan, Malaysia, the Philippines, the ROK, Thailand, Cambodia, and Vietnam are increasingly being used as transit points for illicit consignments of heroin from Southeast Asia destined for Australia, Canada, and the United States, as well as for countries in Europe. It is alarming that the transit countries for heroin from Southeast Asia are on their way to rapidly becoming heroin abusers. In addition to heroin, East and Southeast Asia also pose a major problem due to the illicit manufacture of, traffic in, and abuse of amphetamines. Taiwan remains a major supplier of methamphetamine for Japan, the Philippines, and the ROK, but the illicit manufacture of this drug also takes place in mainland China and Thailand.

In August 1994, to general surprise, the arrest was reported of two North Korean security policemen by Russian authorities on charges of drug trafficking.[33] The two North Koreans were carrying 8.5 kilograms of heroin when they were arrested. This incident actually confirmed a long-standing rumor that North Korea's government is involved in the production of illicit opium and the manufacture and traffic in heroin, simply to earn hard currency. For all these reasons the control of narcotics is increasingly becoming a serious security concern in the Asia Pacific region.

Environmental Degradation.   East Asian countries are beginning to learn how expensive it is to restore the environment once it is damaged as a by-product of the reckless pursuit of rapid industrialization. Acid rain is a common phenomenon; the density of sulfur-oxide compounds in the air far exceeds the world average. River contamination is rapidly drying up sources of potable water, and seawater pollution is rapidly ruining coastal fisheries. Because of the strong external effects or spillover effects of environmental destruction and protection, regionwide cooperative policies and actions are essential. In this regard, the initiative of Northeast Asian countries to regulate seawater contamination is welcome.[34]

Resource Development Disputes.   In addition to disputes over resource development in the South China Sea, potential disputes exist over the development of seabed resources in other waters. In the Yellow Sea, for example, there are latent disputes over mining rights on the continental shelf between China and Korea and between China and Japan. Also reported are clashes between Korean and Chinese fishing boats on the open seas, which possibly reflects potential disputes over fishing rights between the two countries.

Other Nontraditional Security Concerns.   Other possible security concerns include refugee relief, the safeguarding of human rights, and the prevention of international crimes. There are a few potential sources of mass refugees in the region, namely, Hong Kong, Taiwan, and North Korea. The Chinese government repeatedly warns against democratic reforms instituted by the Hong Kong government. If after 1997 China abolishes democratic institutions installed so far in Hong Kong after 1997, this could trigger an exodus. China's invasion of Taiwan and a sudden collapse of North Korea could also give rise to mass refugees. A continued invasion of constitutional rights should not be allowed to prevail. At issue will be the more serious violations of human rights in North Korea and China. Any future regional economic cooperation with those encroaching on human rights should be properly regulated by regional corporate action.

International criminality is still nascent, but some serious crimes have already been reported. Internationally organized crime rings based in Hong Kong were suspected of being involved in the illegal entry of more than 80,000 Chinese into the United States for two years prior to early 1992.[35] The crime rings hired Taiwanese trawlers to carry stowaways for a fare of $50,000 per head. TRIAD, another internationally organized crime ring based in Hong Kong—known for large-scale trafficking of heroin from Southeast Asia to North America and Europe through East Asian transit countries—was reportedly looking for alternative bases to prepare for the return of Hong Kong to China.[36] Consequently, concerned countries are at full alert to prevent TRIAD's entry. There can be no doubt that international organized crimes are on the rise for various reasons in the Asia Pacific region.

Conclusion

In a post-cold war era, varying degrees of uneasiness (from misgivings to apprehension) prevail in East Asia. Broadly speaking there are five variables that have given rise to regional anxiety: a perceived reduction of U.S. forces; the advent of NAFTA; the rapid rise of China; uncertainties surrounding Japan's future identity; and North Korea's nuclear weapons development. These five variables are believed to generate anxiety about nuclear proliferation, a possible new conflict on the Korean peninsula, any emerging future regional security order, the regional economic and trading system, and emerging nontraditional security issues.

From the viewpoint of East Asian countries, almost all of the variables listed above are uncontrollable to varying degrees. This indicates that attempts to maintain the status quo are bound to fail. These countries, however, either out of ignorance, illusion, or sheer selfishness, seem to be tantalizingly slow in making corporate endeavors to address the changed security environment. In a post-cold war era, no country in East Asia will be allowed to be a "free rider." Hence, every country should be prepared to share the legitimate burden to create the stable and peaceful regional security order on which their freedom and prosperity entirely depend.

Notes

1. Kim, Kyung-won, "Korea-U.S. Relationship in Post-Cold War World," *Korea Focus*, April 1994, p. 10. In his excellent paper, Kim analyzes the strategic milieu of East Asia, where the United States finds the tasks of balancing power most complex.

2. U.S. Department of Defense, *A Strategic Framework for the Asian Pacific Rim: Report to Congress* (Washington, D.C., July 1992), 14.

3. Ibid., p. 31.

4. Jonathan D. Pollack, "The United States in East Asia: Holding the Ring," in "Asia's International Role in the Post-Cold War Era, Part I," conference papers, *Adelphi Paper* no. 275, (London: Brassey's for IISS, March 1993), 69.

5. James A. Gregor, "The Clinton Administration's Policy in East Asia," *Global Affairs* (fall 1993): 66.

6. Melvin Gurtov, "The Future of China's Rise," *Asian Perspective* 18, no. 1 (spring-summer 1994): 110.

7. Lucian W. Pye, "Identity and the Political Culture," in Leonard Binder et al., eds., *Crises and Sequences in Political Development* (Princeton, N.J.: Princeton University Press, 1971), 110.

8. S. N. Eisenstadt, "The Breakdown of Communist Regimes and the Vicissitudes of Modernity," *Daedalus* 121 (spring 1992): 28–29. I borrowed the second and third contradictions from him.

9. Such, Dae-Sook, *Kim Il Sung: The North Korean Leader* (New York: Columbia University Press, 1988), 60.

10. Yon, Hyong-muk, Keynote Speech at the fourth round of the inter-Korean Prime Ministers' talks, October 24, 1991, p. 9.

11. Yeo, Yeong-moo, "Testimony of Mr. Ko Yeong-hwan, a Defected ex-North Korean Diplomat," *Shindonga*, November 1991, p. 397.

12. See, for example, Andrew Mack, "North Korea and the Bomb," *Foreign Policy*, no. 83 (summer 1991): 99; William Epstein, "Nuclear Security for the Korean Peninsula," *Korean Journal of Defense Analysis* 4, no. 2 (winter 1992): 56–57; and Darryl Howlett, "Nuclearization or Denuclearization on the Korean Peninsula," *Contemporary Security Policy* 15, no. 2 (August 1994): 184.

13. Kim Il Sung, "10-point Program of Great Unity of the Whole Nation for Reunification of the Country," *Rodongshinmun*, April 7, 1993.

14. Some scholars misleadingly argue that North Korea may have been highly motivated to obtain its own nuclear weapons by its deteriorating international and domestic military and political position relative to that of South Korea. See, for example, Peter Hayes, *Pacific Powderkeg* (Lexington, Mass.: Lexington Books, 1990), 212.

15. Les Aspin, Secretary of Defense, *Annual Report to the President and the Congress*, January 1994, p. 9.

16. Ezra F. Vogel, "Japanese-American Relations After the Cold War," *Daedalus* 121 (fall 1992): 38.

17. Bernard Herber, *Modern Public Finance* (Homewood, Ill.: Richard D. Irwin, Inc., 1967), 24.

18. Fu Zhengyuan, "Continuities of Chinese Political Tradition," *Studies of Comparative Communism* 24, no. 3 (September 1991): 262.

19. Gerald Segal, "As China Grows Strong," *International Affairs* 64, no. 2 (spring 1988): 231. Segal, however, presents more relaxed views later. See his more recent essay, "China's Changing Shape," *Foreign Affairs* 73, no. 3 (May/June 1994): 43 -58. See also, James R. Lilley, "American Security in Asia," *Global Affairs* (fall 1993): 75; Monte R. Bullard, "US-China Relations: The Strategic Calculus," *Parameter* (summer 1993): 93; Huang Yasheng, "China's Economic Development: Implications for its Political and Security Roles," in *Adelphi Paper* no. 275, p. 57; Gregor, "The Clinton Administration's Policy in East Asia," 63–65; Gurtov, "The Future of China's Rise," 124–126; Richard Mansbach, "The New Order in Northeast Asia: A Theoretical Overview," *Asian Perspective* 17, no. 1 (spring-summer 1993): 11–13; and Harry Harding, "China at the Crossroads: Conservatism, Reform or Decay?" in *Adelphi Paper* no. 275, p. 48.

20. Hideo Sato, "Japan's Role in the Post-Cold War World," *Current History* 90, no. 555 (April 1991): 145.

21. Ibid., 147–148.

22. Peter J. Katzenstein and Nobuo Okawara, "Japan's National Security," *International Security* 17, no. 4 (spring 1993): 86.

23. Sato, "Japan's Role," 146.

24. *U.S. News & World Report*, August 22, 1994, p. 48.

25. Vogel, "Japanese-American Relations," 45.

26. Stuart Harris, "The Economic Aspects of Pacific Security," in *Adelphi Paper* no. 275, pp. 18–19.

27. Ibid., 21.

28. *Far Eastern Economic Review,* May 28, 1992, p. 23.

29. *Kyung-Hyang Shinmun,* July 4, 1992, p. 5.

30. *Chosun Ilbo,* March 22, 1994, p. 8.

31. Carl W. Ford Jr., "Key Strategic and Security Issues in East Asia: The China Factor" (Paper presented at the Conference on the Clinton Administration's Policy toward the PRC and Taiwan, sponsored by the Center for East Asian Studies, the Pennsylvania State University, and the Taiwan Institute for Political, Economic and Strategic Studies, at the Gaston Sigur Center, George Washington University, February 5, 1994), 13.

32. United Nations, *Report of the International Narcotics Control Board for 1993,* 39–40.

33. *Hankook Ilbo,* Aug. 6, 1994.

34. Ibid., Jan. 10, 1994.

35. Ibid., March 23, 1992, p. 10.

36. *Segyae Ilgo,* Jan. 12, 1994, p. 23.

4

Asia Pacific Security Concerns:
A Singaporean Perspective

Kwa Chong Guan

During the past 40 years, the issues and challenges that preoccupied the nations of Southeast Asia were fairly well defined. We were either part of the group of states seeking to change the world through revolution or part of the other group of states attempting to contain revolutionary change. Some among us attempted to be part of neither group, to be non-aligned..Today, with the demolition of the Berlin Wall and the dissolution of the Soviet Union, these old divides and structures are irrelevant. We have to reconstruct our world and identify the new issues that are challenging our efforts to build a new world. Some of us are searching for trends and forces that we can project into the future. Others are more speculatively exploring what kind of Southeast Asia and wider Asia Pacific we would like to live in during the twenty-first century. We construct different visions and scenarios of the future and attempt an analysis of how plausible they are.

Memories and Scenarios

Key to this planning of scenarios are our assumptions about the kind of world in which we want to live and our perception of our present reality. These assumptions are rooted in personal memories and the memories of the family and community to which we belong. Our social memories form a framework for defining and unifying the group and community and for responding to the world. Social memories influence our choices of what is desirable and our assessment of what is feasible. We make our memory, and our memory makes us.

Our social memories guide us toward two scenarios for the region in the twenty-first century. The elements of an optimistic scenario would include the following:

- The United States remains economically and politically committed to the region, helping to underpin regional stability.

- The Asia Pacific Economic Cooperation (APEC) forum takes off and provides the institutional framework for continuing U.S. economic commitment and investments.

- The U.S.-Japan relationship remains strong. (Asian economic growth and regional stability have, to a large extent, been premised on an economically powerful but militarily dependent Japan, whose security is defined by an American-drafted constitution and an American-backed bilateral security treaty.)

- A post-Deng collective leadership proves capable of holding China together on its current course of economic development.

- A framework is set up (perhaps the East Asia Economic Caucus) for cooperative economic relations between Southeast Asia and China's Special Economic Zones.

- Japan increases its direct investment in Southeast Asia, which would continue to expand as Japan opens its domestic markets to Southeast Asian products.

- Regionalism continues to grow apace, coexisting under a framework of globalism.

- The region experiences intensified deregulation, privatization, growth triangles (linking north Malaysian states, southern Thailand, and north Sumatra or Brunei with Sulawesi and the southern Philippines), and private sector initiatives that enhance its economic integration and growth.

What, however, is the future of the region if globalism, open regionalism, nondiscriminatory trade, and continuing economic growth are not sustained? A pessimistic scenario for the region would include the following elements:

- Domestic U.S. economic pressures increase, leading to a reduction of the U.S. military presence in the Asia Pacific region, a tougher approach toward redressing the trade deficit with Japan (which would further strain U.S.-Japan relations), and decreasing U.S. economic involvement in Southeast Asia.

- Japan moves away from the United States and becomes an independent military power.

- Two trading blocs emerge: the European Union, extended to include eastern Europe and parts of the old Soviet Union west of the Urals; and an Asia Pacific group centered around a yen bloc.

- A leadership succession crisis occurs in North Korea that spills over and destabilizes Northeast Asia.

- A leadership succession crisis befalls China, leading to economic collapse and political crisis.

- Prolonged economic recession or political crises beset the region, which would threaten the fragile civil society in many countries.

This chapter explores some of the assumptions underlying these two scenarios. Common and central to both scenarios are the attitudes and policies of the major external powers—China, Japan, and the United States—toward the nations of Southeast Asia. The memories of how China, Japan and the United States previously responded to and treated the nations of Southeast Asia will influence future expectations. The challenge is that there are multiple memories that often contradict one another and, when translated into policy, may align the nations of Southeast Asia against one another. More significantly, memories evolve in response to the present. What we recall of, and how we assess today, the U.S. Marine landing near Da Nang on March 8, 1965, may differ—only slightly, but perhaps significantly—from what we remembered and our assessment in 1965. Memories change and evolve in response to the world around us and the people and groups with whom we interact. The challenge is to ensure that the interaction of our memories leads to a world that is more secure and peaceful than the present.

Legacies of a Plural Society

For many of us, our memories of ourselves as nation-states are fairly short. For most members of the Association of Southeast Asian Nations (ASEAN), the memory of winning independence from colonial powers is still living. Our colonial past continues to be a part of our present. In Singapore we still live with our colonial legacy of sojourners and immigrants attracted to this British colonial entrepôt. Here we eked out a living within what the British colonial administrator J. S. Furnival termed a "plural society," describing the discrete ethnic groups resident in a British colony that met and interacted primarily in the market place. Outside the market, the different communities of a plural society retreated into their separate enclaves to live out their different lifestyles. It is a history that, as Furnival pointed out, is replicated in British Malaya, Burma, and the Dutch East Indies.

The consequence of this legacy is that we recognize that the social glue that holds the disparate ethnic groups, trading minorities, religious congregations, and other communities together as a civil society in a nation-state is weak. We are very aware of the fragility of our civil society, which can so easily disintegrate into ethnic and religious strife, secessionist movements, and antigovernment unrest—unless the government of the day can rise above sectarian interests to impose some form of control perceived to be fair and acceptable to the disaggregated groups making up the state.

Most of us are, therefore, extremely sensitive toward any challenge or development threatening the fragility of our civil society. We are aware that the process of modernization, far from moderating and eroding ethnic consciousness, on the contrary, may exacerbate it. And, in today's increasingly borderless world, we recognize that external forces and influences challenge our domestic development and stability. When we scan the horizon for such challenges, we detect other states in the region with equally, if not more fragile, civil societies. We are concerned because we recognize that in the post-cold war era, wars are more likely to be triggered by intercommunal violence than by territorial aggression fueled by ideology.

The reality today is that the prototypical conflict is now a function of a weak state. Political tensions, economic inequalities, religious differences, and ethnic conflicts can lead to breakdowns of law and order, to secessionist movements, and to civil war. Any breakdown of civil society can in today's borderless world spill over to affect others in the region. Currently the sustained economic growth we are enjoying holds our potentially fragile societies together. But what if growth is not sustained?

The events and developments that will shape the integrity of our civil society include the political stability and economic growth, not only of our own countries, but of the region as a whole (and especially of our neighbors). Other developments that will shape us include the shrinking of the U.S. deficit, the continuity of the U.S.-Japan alliance, and the post-Deng economic and political stability of China.

Huaqiao to Huaren

A major challenge to the post-colonial transformation of our pluralistic societies has been the economic disparities between the Chinese and other indigenous communities. Ignored by the Qing rulers of China, Chinese migrants to Southeast Asia from the seventeenth century to the end of the nineteenth century had to be self-sufficient and independent. They became an increasingly successful "trading minority" in the region. Unfortunately, assimilation of the Chinese into new civil societies was complicated and became a major political issue. Allegiances and loyalties were called into question because the remembered past indicated they might lie elsewhere.

The May 4th Movement introduced a new political discourse disseminated by reformers and revolutionaries to mobilize the people, including those who had migrated. Overseas Chinese, or *huaqiao*, neglected and ignored by the Qing, were now recognized and exhorted to remember their "ancestral homeland" (*zuguo*). Both Sun Yat-sen and Kang Youwei traveled the region canvassing *huaqiao* support. The *huaqiao* were encouraged to perceive themselves as constituents of a large and scattered, but unified, "imagined community" or *minzu*. Such appeals created an identity crisis among the overseas Chinese, dividing the community. In contrast to more recent immigrants who responded to China's needs, older immigrants who had lost their ties with their ancestral homeland and whose political point of reference had shifted to their adopted homeland were not moved by the *huaqiao* ideology. Tan Kah Kee, one of the most prominent industrial capitalists of colonial Singapore, still remains our most prominent example of a *huaqiao* who carried his ideology to its logical conclusion and became a "Returned Overseas Chinese" (*guiqiao*) when he left Singapore for the newly founded People's Republic of China in 1950.

Our memory of this *huaqiao* legacy is complicated by another set of relationships established by the Chinese Communist Party (CCP) with fraternal parties in the region. Inspired by the CCP revolutionary seizure of power and encouraged by an imperious Chinese government after 1949, these fraternal Communist parties in some cases launched protracted armed struggles to seize power. The CCP, after breaking with the Soviets at their Eighth Party Congress in 1956, successfully moved to establish itself as the leader of an Asian anti-Soviet bloc of Communist parties. With the exception of former Indochina, social memories of these abortive attempts by Southeast Asian Communist parties to seize power remain fresh and vivid. Neither the Malaysians nor the Indonesians are likely to forget the Emergency of GESTAPU generated by the coup attempt in Indonesia in 1965. ASEAN as a group will remember for some time Chinese support for Pol Pot and his Khmers Rouges. These social memories will influence our perception of China, especially for as long as it remains one of the last Leninist states.

Today, Deng's Four Modernizations have transformed Mao Tse-tung's revolutionary China. But this transformation has been with the help of the *guiquao* whom China has been wooing and direct foreign investments from Chinese in Hong Kong, Macau, Taiwan, and Southeast Asia. This successful wooing of investments from overseas Chinese generates a number of concerns, if not dilemmas.

First, are these investments in China a response to new business and economic opportunities (i.e., an economics-driven decision) or part of a globalization of Chinese big business in Southeast Asia? Or, more insidiously, are they a consequence of a reviving *huaqiao* ideology? Senior Minister Lee Kuan Yew of Singapore addressed this issue when he spoke to an international convention of World Chinese Entrepreneurs in August 1991. Noting that "our world is increasingly interdependent," Lee conceded that "ethnic and cultural empathy facilitates rapport and trust." But others in the region were suspicious and unhappy, and the absence of leading Indonesian entrepreneurs like Liem Sioe Liong, William Soeryadjaya, and Ciputra is indicative. Senior Minister Lee, apparently aware of this unhappiness, warned in his address to the second World Chinese Entrepreneurs Convention in Hong Kong in November 1993 that Chinese entrepreneurs who come from "certain sensitive

ASEAN countries should take care that their investments in their own countries do not diminish as a result of their China investments." Lee noted that "if relations turn sour between any ASEAN country and China, those ethnic Chinese who have invested in China will be accused of disloyalty."

Second, should Southeast Asian Chinese entrepreneurs be helping to build a "Great Chinese Economic Zone" that in the longer term could lead to a strong and prosperous China with the capability to dominate the region economically and wield extraordinary political and military influence? On the other hand, can Southeast Asian Chinese big business afford *not* to invest in China? Both Wong Kan Seng, then Singapore foreign minister, in his address, and Professor Wang Gungwu, in his keynote lecture, at an International Conference on Southeast Asian Chinese in Singapore on January 21, 1994, stressed that investments in China by Chinese entrepreneurs in Southeast Asia, Hong Kong, or Taiwan were not governed by emotions and kinship, but based on hard business calculations of profits and returns on investments.

The possibility that an economically strong China could support an imperious and militarily threatening China is the worse-case scenario we carry in our memory. China's naval modernization programs, which could eventually provide a blue-water capability, raise images of a twenty-first century Zheng He sailing through the Straits of Melaka. Zheng He occupies a fairly prominent place in our social memories. A lead exhibit in the Melaka history museum recreates in a life-size tableau Zheng He and his entourage kneeling before the Soltan of Melaka, while temples to his honor stand in Melaka and Semarang. China's February 1992 legislation claiming most of the South China Sea as Chinese waters is a source of continuing concern about how China perceives or could treat us.

Ultimately, Southeast Asian concerns with China must come to focus on the implications and consequences of a "Greater China" (*dazhonghua*). The economies of China, especially in the special economic zones, Hong Kong, and Taiwan, are becoming increasingly interlinked and involve Southeast Asian Chinese big business as well. What will be the implications of a growing transnational Chinese economy for our national economies? Coupled with this transnational Chinese economy is the creation of a "pan-Chinese culture" (*fan Zhonghuaxing wenhua*), the contents of which may be diffused but still appear to be attracting and engaging an increasing number of Chinese overseas.

What will be the consequences of this evolving "pan-Chinese culture" on our civil societies?

Finally, what are the visions of China's post-Deng leaders as to the type of China they will inherit? Southeast Asians will have to live with the consequences of these visions, as our remembered past instructs. In 1432, the third Ming emperor mothballed the great fleets and moved the imperial capital to Beijing, committing his successors to construction of a Great Wall. It will remain one of the great "ifs" of our history whether China would have colonized our world had the Ming vision not turned inward. Southeast Asians would probably not have experienced an Age of Commerce from the fourteenth to the eighteenth century, had the inward shift not occurred.

Pax Nipponica?

Compared to China, our memories of Japan are much shorter, but no less complex. The Japanese invasion and three-and-a-half-year occupation of Southeast Asia was a turning point in our history. The Allies found their return challenged by nationalist movements that declared or were demanding independence. But the older generation has not forgotten, nor have some forgiven, the Japanese for their actions. They consider Japan's failure to acknowledge past atrocities arrogant and wrong.

Saburo Ienaga's 30-year lawsuit against the Japanese Ministry of Education's attempt to get him to change his assessments in his school textbook on Japan's actions in World War II—which the court decided in his favor in May 1994—is the tip of an iceberg of controversy over Japanese atrocities during the war. Ienaga is in the minority challenging Japanese history textbook accounts of Japan's 15-year invasion and occupation of China and Southeast Asia. He is prepared to describe Japanese actions as "aggression," but the Japanese Ministry of Education disagrees and wants to emphasize instead patriotism and State Shinto. Shigeto Nagano, the Japanese minister of justice who was forced to resign in May 1994 for his comments denying that a massacre occurred in Nanjing, may have been correctly expressing a point of view subscribed to by the Liberal Democratic Party and other more nationalistic groups in Japan. It is a point of view the Chinese, Koreans, and others have objected to and formally protested to Japan.

A number of us in the region are concerned over the implications of Japan's refusal to acknowledge its activities in World

War II, unlike the Germans. Japanese historians have yet to go through the cathartic *Historikerstreit* (historians' dispute) that German historians went through in the 1980s. A generation or more of Japanese appear unaware of their country's activities in World War II. Former prime minister Toshiki Kaifu admitted this when he expressed "sincere contrition for Japanese past actions which inflicted unbearable suffering and sorrow upon a great many people of the Asia Pacific region." He stated that he was "determined to step up our efforts to ensure that today's young people—tomorrow's leaders—gain a full and accurate under- standing of modern and contemporary Japanese history through their education in schools and in society at large."

For some of us in ASEAN, a younger generation of Japanese ignorant of their past, combined with a leadership unrepentant over their conduct in the war, is a source of concern, especially when that leadership is in command of a Self-Defense Force that now has the second largest military budget in the world. At this time, the United States and its treaty with Japan are reassuring— but for how much longer?

The seven-year American occupation transformed Japan from an enemy to a cold war ally. National Security Council paper 48/1 proposed "a strategic offense in the 'West' and a stra- tegic defense in the 'East' in which Japan would have a pivotal role." NSC 48/1 concluded by suggesting that this objective of containing communism could be achieved by accelerating the integration of Japan's economy with that of Southeast Asia. This Japan has achieved today with massive U.S. aid in the interven- ing 45 years. In effect, the United States, wittingly or unwit- tingly, has aided Japan in recreating its Greater East Asian Co- prosperity Sphere. But this was a strategic reality most of us in the region accepted.

Japan is today the largest foreign aid donor to ASEAN. In 1990, Japan's Overseas Development Aid to ASEAN totaled some U.S.\$2.2 billion. Japanese direct investments in ASEAN in 1990 totaled some U.S.\$3.2 billion, nearly six times more than in 1985, when a new wave of investments started moving into the region. Prior to 1985, Japanese investments were primarily in resource extraction and import substitution. Appreciation of the yen following the Plaza Agreement of 1985 forced Japanese corporations to relocate their export-oriented industries out of Japan. ASEAN economies, attempting to break out of import substitution strategies and seeking new capital inflows to help relieve the debt burden, welcomed these new Japanese investments, as evidenced in Malaysia's "Look East" policy. But these new investments have not been without cost. Japan's *keiretsu* system of families of companies, each holding stock in the others and moving as a bloc, has meant that Japanese foreign investments are often within the family. Thus an automobile manufacturer may come in with its assembly plant, its family of component suppliers, a bank, and a trading company. Local manufacturers, banks, and trading companies are involved as dependents of the Japanese, rather than in a complementary relationship. Such investment practices do not lead to happy memories.

For the United States, the cost of helping Japan to achieve this level of economic progress (while also providing a security umbrella) has been high. From the late 1960s, Japan started to register a trade surplus and the United States a trade deficit. The strategic equation of supporting Japan as the cost of winning allies to contain China and the Soviets in the cold war was starting to crack. The initial assessment was that this trade inversion was a temporary aberration, but it did not correct itself; in fact, it has widened and persisted. Differences over what could be done proved intractable and threatened to lead to economic conflict. ASEAN watched with growing concern as differences developed between the United States and Japan. The ASEAN states find Japan a discomforting and difficult trading and economic partner and an unacceptable political and security leader. If we have to choose between the United States and Japan, then the choice is not between two different capitalist systems, but between two visions for the Asia Pacific. One goes back to the Meiji restoration, the other to the American Revolution. If we have to make a choice, our social memories make it clear where our choice will be.

The United States: Lost Hegemony

Our memories of the United States are, like our memories of Japan, short and, with the possible exception of the Philippines, somewhat ambivalent. We have positive memories of American efforts to persuade its allies not to reestablish their colonial empires in the region at the end of World War II. But our subsequent memories of U.S. efforts to embroil us in the escalating cold war are more ambivalent. With the exception of Thailand and the Philippines, we avoided the Southeast Asia Treaty Organization, even though a nascent Indonesian Republic had experienced an abortive coup by the Indonesian Community Party (PKI) in 1947 and Malaya was combatting an armed Communist insurgency. The Bandung Conference in 1955 was an effort by a number of ASEAN states to steer a path between the cold war camps, for we still recalled that it was not only China and its local Communist parties that could challenge and threaten us, but also the United States. The United States expected us to subscribe to its foreign policy objectives as a consequence of being on its side of the effort to contain communism. Where compliance was not forthcoming, the United States threatened, and in some cases attempted to impose, change in our countries according to its dictates.

Today, at the end of the cold war, our image of the United States is of a country with chronic trade and current account deficits, internally divided and slipping. Paul Kennedy's 1987 bestseller, *The Rise and Fall of the Great Powers*, appears to corroborate our impression that the United States is in decline because of "imperial overstretch." A steadily declining U.S. defense budget, which by 1997 will be down an estimated 35 percent from the 1985 level, appears to be partly a consequence of this "imperial overstretch" and partly the result of strategic drift. The present and preceding U.S. administrations' visions of Asia appear to still betray a cold war mind-set. With the dissolution of the Soviet military presence in the region, the raison d'être for a corresponding U.S. military presence breaks down.

U.S. economic and political power may have declined relative to the late 1940s and early 1950s. The United States may have a chronic trade deficit. But its corporations continue to be world leaders. The top *Fortune* 500 companies are big not only in the United States but globally. They may not be able to compete in the manufacture of consumer goods, but these are "sunset" industries; what counts is to be in the forefront of research and development of tomorrow's technology, an area in which U.S. multinationals lead. Overall, the "competitive advantage," as defined by Michael Porter, may still lie with U.S. corporations.

It is, however, the continuing premier position of the U.S. dollar that gives Washington a dominant influence over the structure of international finance and credit. As long as we continue to transact our international finances in U.S. dollars, we grant to the United States the modern equivalent of the medieval privilege of seigniorage, the right of rulers to issue legal tender and to profit from its issue. Few, if any, among us can issue more currency to cover our deficits in government spending and foreign trade and, in doing so, pass on to our trading partners the cost of our extravagance. Only the United States could have got away with a unilateral 1971 decision to abandon a long-standing commitment on the convertibility of its dollar into gold. Our perceptions of the United States in decline may therefore be erroneous. What we may be witnessing instead is a swing of U.S. public opinion toward introspection, as happened between World War I and World War II.

Our current impressions of U.S. preoccupation with debt sharing and variations on collective security and multilateralism as a consequence of cutting costs may be incorrect. These U.S. preoccupations may be more the consequence of a continuing Wilsonian legacy in international relations. The challenge for us in ASEAN may then be to come to terms with this Wilsonian legacy in U.S. international relations.

Changing Social Memories

The implosion of the Soviet Union took place faster than we anticipated. The fallout of this implosion is spreading wider than we initially feared. China's four modernizations have transformed the country, and especially the coastal region, faster than Beijing wants or can control. The challenge is for our social memories to recognize and register these accelerating changes. It will be a disaster if we unconsciously continue to register and interpret the fast-changing strategic environment with cold war mind-sets. Today we must search for new forms of security cooperation structured around various confidence and security building measures. The issues confronting the search involve not only the substance of what is to be negotiated, but also the style of negotiations.

If we compare Asia to Europe, we see that a style and format for diplomatic negotiations has evolved in Europe since the Treaty of Westphalia. In Asia, however, social memories continue to be expressed in very different styles of rhetoric. Within ASEAN we in Singapore understand that our Indonesian partners have fairly different communicative styles that also differ from our Thai, Malaysian, Brunei, and Filipino partners. But we have been together long enough to evolve an ASEAN style. As we seek to expand security cooperation we have to engage other codes and styles of communication. We have, for example, to learn to sort out the *tatemae* terms our Japanese colleagues may address to us, and the *honne* (his or her actual intentions) that may be deeply embedded in their *tatemae* phrases. Perhaps our fundamental concern should be whether our memories can keep pace with the change around us—whether we can be flexible enough to adapt to the different strategic cultures we now have to traverse.

5

A Survey of Confidence and Security Building Measures

M. Susan Pederson and Stanley Weeks

Growing interest in the development of confidence and security building measures (CSBMs) for the Asia Pacific reflects a number of factors: increasing concern about post-cold war security structures; growing apprehension about the pace and extent of U.S. withdrawals; the emergence of an increasingly mature Association of Southeast Asian Nations (ASEAN) committed to promoting regionwide security dialogue; and activism by United Nations (UN) disarmament bodies in pushing regional arms control agendas.

Although such developments have focused increased attention on CSBMs, the future role of such measures in promoting a regional security agenda is far from clear. The Asia Pacific differs in important respects from areas of the world where CSBMs have prospered. The region is more geographically, politically, and culturally diverse than any other in which confidence building efforts have been pursued. Perhaps most important, although troubled by some of the world's most explosive hot spots, the Asia Pacific as a whole is characterized less by actively adversarial relationships than by the potential for conflict. Territorial disputes, competing economic and resource interests, and lingering domestic insecurities suggest the need for measures aimed at averting the rise of tension and conflict. CSBMs, by contrast, have been most commonly developed and applied to assist in dismantling confrontational or actively hostile situations.

The nature of the Asia Pacific security environment has led some to argue the futility of transferring European or other CSBM experience to Asia, or to suggest a new approach to confidence building emphasizing economic and social dimensions.[1]

The authors would like to thank Anne Uchitel and Brian Connors of SAIC for their assistance in developing the research and ideas contained in this paper.

A competing perspective argues that although the experience of each region is to some extent unique, a careful reading of the record of current CSBMs, especially in Europe, may yield generic lessons relevant elsewhere.[2]

This chapter takes the latter view and considers current and past experience with CSBMs in Europe and other regions in order to address the answers to two questions:

- What are confidence building measures, and does a new understanding of the concept or a new term for the measures need to be defined?

- What is the historical record of CSBM implementation, and what lessons can be drawn from the apparent success or failure of measures that have been applied in Europe, South Asia, Latin America, and currently the Middle East?

Combined with an assessment of broad security trends and issues in the Asia Pacific, the answers to such questions may suggest the potential relevance of different CSBMs to the security problems of the region.

Definitions

Definitions of CSBMs are many and varied.[3] In the broadest sense, CSBMs could include "a myriad of political, economic, and environmental arrangements which are themselves not concerned with security, but which in sum indirectly probably contribute more to regional confidence and security than those measures specifically designed for that purpose."[4] As evolved in Western and other practice, however, confidence building measures have referred more narrowly to initiatives addressing military planning and operational activity. To cite one concise definition: "Confidence building involves the credible evidence of the absence of feared threats. . . . A major objective of CBMs is to provide reassurance by reducing uncertainties and by constraining opportunities for exerting pressure through military activity."[5]

In this definition, CSBMs are measures that tend to make military intentions more explicit by increasing transparency and predictability, thus reducing the risk of war by accident or miscalculation. In more ambitious and constraining forms, CSBMs are also measures that reduce the possibility of surprise attack or, in crises, give greater warning of impending attack. They achieve these objectives by giving states greater information about other nations' military activities and doctrine, or by constraining military operations. Such measures, however, are not arms limitation measures in the strictest sense: they do not limit force levels and they typically do not carry the weight of legally binding treaties, although they can and have set the stage for formal limitation efforts.[6]

Nor should CSBMs be regarded as synonymous with either comprehensive security frameworks or cooperative/joint defense arrangements. Although CSBMs can form one element of comprehensive security frameworks (which, like the European CSCE and Middle East Multilateral Peace Processes, treat both military and non-military aspects of security comprehensively), CSBMs do not themselves combine political, economic, and social dimensions. With regard to cooperative/joint defense arrangements, the focus of CSBMs is on limiting or clarifying military activities that may be perceived as threatening rather than prescribing activities that contribute to joint defense.

An argument is sometimes made for adopting a broader conception of CSBMs in the Asia Pacific, but there may be some virtue in retaining a narrow definition. A strict definition may permit greater focus on efforts to defuse the military sources of conflict and to achieve concrete and measurable implementation results. The relatively profitable record of CSBMs in Europe, where the West successfully resisted Soviet efforts to broaden and thus dilute such measures, may argue for similar resolve in Asia. Moreover, a narrow definition does not preclude parallel efforts to achieve greater economic or humanitarian cooperation or to develop joint defense cooperation in separate or related forums. Both the CSCE and Middle East experiences illustrate this point.

Arguing that CSBMs are most useful when concretely focused, however, does not imply that "confidence building" is necessarily the only or best term to apply to such efforts. Just as measures themselves must be tailored to reflect regional realities, so their titles can be adapted to reflect regional sensitivities. Whether labeled mutual reassurance measures, trust-building measures, CSBMs, CBMs, or some variant, what distinguishes these initiatives is the emphasis on illuminating, clarifying, and sometimes constraining the military activity of neighboring states.

Typologies of CSBMs are as varied as their definitions. In general, however, measures fall into one of three broad categories: *declaratory measures*—statements of intent including broad

Chart 5.1
Declaratory Measures

Briand-Kellogg Pact renouncing war (1928)

Soviet nuclear no-first-use pledges

Indo-Pakistani Simla Accord (1971), renouncing force

Helsinki Final Act (1975), acceptance of existing borders

December 1991 ROK-DPRK agreements, non-attack and
  nuclear-free peninsula pledges

Negative Security Assurances (NSA), pledging no nuclear
  attack of non-nuclear powers

---

commitments such as non-attack or no-first-use agreements
(chart 5.1); *transparency measures*—including information, communication, notification, and observation/inspection measures
(chart 5.2); and *constraint measures*—including risk reduction
regimes and exclusion/separation zones, as well as more traditional constraints on personnel, equipment, and operational
activities (chart 5.3). Such measures can be implemented as unilateral, bilateral, or multilateral initiatives (in the latter case with
global, regional, or subregional application), and adopted as a
result of formal negotiations or informal agreement with or without legal force. Further, CSBMs can be applied in varying
degrees to either conventional forces or nuclear, biological,
chemical, and missile capabilities.

How successful have such measures been? Which initiatives
have worked and which have not? Any effort to discern the lessons learned from CSBMs to date has to generalize across a
record that is often ambiguous, contradictory, and incomplete. In
making judgments, it helps to recognize that the success of such
measures lies not only in the degree to which they have
enhanced transparency and lessened mistrust—outcomes that
are hard to prove in any event—but also in the degree to which
CSBMs, because they were successfully negotiated and implemented, contributed to patterns of routine communication and
cooperation that themselves helped to lessen tension and promote mutual reassurance.

Chart 5.2
Transparency Measures

Information Measures

- Defense White Paper publication
- Calendar of military activities
- Exchanges of military data
- Military-to-military contacts
- Doctrine/defense planning seminars

- Arms registry
- Military personnel/ student exchanges
- NBCM[a] material inventories
- NBCM facilities

Communication Measures

- Crisis management (hotlines)
- Conflict Prevention Centers (CPCs)
- Multilateral communications network
- Mandatory consultation on unusual/dangerous activities

- Communication for unexplained nuclear incidents
- Obligatory consultations in situations with increased nuclear war risk

Notification Measures

- Military maneuvers/movements
- Military alerts
- Increase in personnel (ground/ air)

- Call-up of reserves
- Test missile launches
- Nuclear accidents

Observation/Inspection Measures

- Invitation of observers
- Surveillance and control zones
- Open skies
- Troop separation and monitoring

- Sensors/early warning stations
- Nuclear missile factories
- Nuclear missile destruction
- Chemical facilities

---

[a] Nuclear, biological, chemical, and missile

Assessments of CSBM success, however, must take into account the varied record of different regions. What has worked in one region at one time may be fundamentally out of place in others. Reviewing the post-World War II record of implementation suggests the points of convergence and divergence, as well as the conditions underpinning successful confidence building efforts.

Chart 5.3
Constraint Measures

Risk Reduction Measures

- Agreement to Reduce Risk of Nuclear War (1971)
- Incidents at Sea Agreement (1972)
- Russo-Japanese Air Traffic Safety Agreement (1985)
- Nuclear Risk Reduction Center Agreement (1987)
- Dangerous Military Activities Agreement (1989)

Exclusion/Separation Measures

- Demilitarized zones
- Disengagement zones
- Keep-out zones (air/sea)
- NBCM-free zones

Constraints on Personnel, Equipment, Activities

Personnel
- National limits
- Category limits
- Zone limits

Equipment
- Deployment limits (by geographic area or numbers)
- Category/type limits
- Storage/monitoring limits
- Nuclear missile types/deployment

Activities
- Maneuvers/movements limits, by size or geographic area
- Advance notification for movements, exercises, alerts
- Limits on readiness
- Bans on simultaneous exercises/alerts and/or certain force/unit types
- NBCM testing
- Nuclear fissile material production constraints

A Regional Survey of CSBMs

The modern experience of CSBMs dates from competing U.S. and Soviet proposals at the UN in the early 1950s for "open sky" and ground post observation in Europe. Although themselves a failure, these initiatives provided an indirect prelude to more serious, and ultimately more successful, U.S.-Soviet confidence building efforts in the aftermath of the Cuban missile crisis. Focused initially on crisis communications and later on risk reduction, these efforts led over 25 years to a series of agreements intended to contain nuclear crises, to establish rules of routine military conduct at sea and on land, and to create mechanisms for joint crisis management.[7] Helping in the early period to set the stage for arms control efforts, at later stages these confidence building activities provided a forum for continuing dialogue in the face of worsening relations. Thus, although themselves modest in scope and intent, U.S.-Soviet CSBMs played a crucial role in opening and sustaining communication at critical points in the evolving superpower relationship.

By the early 1970s, U.S.-Soviet détente had helped to set the stage for European confidence building efforts in the Conference on Security and Cooperation in Europe (1971–1975). Few anticipated in 1975 that the modest notification and observation provisions of the Helsinki Final Act would lead over the course of 15 years to a progressively more complete series of notification, information exchange, and constraining measures, or that such measures would move from the limited objectives of enhancing transparency and predictability to the more ambitious goal of limiting the potential for surprise attack and politically coercive uses of force.

Nor did observers predict the nature or extent of the dramatic transformation of European relations that occurred over the same period. The role of CSBMs in prompting such changes is, of course, debatable. Certainly, CSBMs in place in 1980 did not stop the Soviets from using the threat of force to coerce the Polish crackdown on Solidarity. Nor is there experience to suggest that the constraint measures negotiated at Stockholm would necessarily have been more effective. What CSBMs did, however, was to foster communication and cooperation in a way that helped to regulate East-West competition and contain tensions that arose. Although only one of many factors contributing to this outcome, their positive impact was no less salient.

The CSCE process has provided the best known and most extensive experience, but recent initiatives in other regions have disseminated these measures more widely. In Latin America, conventional CSBMs have been adopted as part of the Contadora peace process and in the resolution of the Falklands dispute. Argentina and Brazil have shared information and mutual inspections of their respective nuclear programs, and most nations in the region abide by the nuclear-free aspirations of the Treaty of Tlatelolco. The Organization of American States (OAS) Governmental Experts' meeting in March 1994 resulted in an illustrative list of CSBMs for countries to consider adopting and agreement that a Regional Conference on CSBMs in Latin America would be held in 1995.[8]

In South Asia, India and Pakistan have turned to CSBMs, often under Western pressure, to promote crisis disengagement, improve communications, and make routine force maneuvers more predictable. Including an extensive array of communication, notification, observation, and disengagement zone measures, these CSBMs have enjoyed a mixed record of implementation, with reported violations going unresolved as a lingering point of contention.

More successful in Asia have been Sino-Indian, Russian-Japanese, and more recently Sino-Russian initiatives, in which a spirit of practical cooperation on a range of communication, notification, and incidents at sea measures appears to prevail. The recent announcement of plans for India and China to hold joint military exercises in the summer of 1995 reveals the extent of progress in this area.[9]

Of greatest recent interest as a model of regional confidence building is the Middle East Multilateral Peace Process, in which Israel and a number of Arab states are considering a range of CSBM initiatives under multinational sponsorship. Slowly gathering momentum since its inception in 1991, the Multilateral Working Group on Arms Control and Regional Security (ACRS) has made progress toward defining a regional confidence building agenda that focuses on crisis management and defusing tensions at the edge of war. Like early U.S.-Soviet efforts, significant interest appears to lie in the establishment of communication networks and in defining rules of naval conduct. But although the substantive focus of this initial dialogue may resemble early East-West initiatives, the modalities of the ACRS process reflect the unique political, cultural, and historical experience of the region.

Divided by centuries of religious animosity and mistrust and lacking practical experience of arms control, Middle East participants are being formally mentored in their confidence building by third nations, which have taken the lead in identifying prospective initiatives, describing modalities, and conducting demonstrations of selected measures in practice, for example, by hosting regional observers at search and rescue exercises.

Such efforts are consistent with the prominent role outside parties have traditionally played in the political and military affairs of the region and reflect recent experience with third-party enforcement of disengagement zones in the Sinai and the Golan Heights. As all parties recognize, however, gaining eventual regional ownership of proposed measures will be the critical test of whether such efforts will ultimately succeed, notwithstanding the constructive role mentors may play at the present stage.

Some common themes emerge from this review of regional confidence building experience. Clearly, successful security dialogue requires a general appreciation that the benefits of accommodation outweigh the interests of continued conflict. Confidence building has thus often been precipitated by events—whether crises or shifts in geopolitical alignment—that make accommodation desirable. Given such opportunities, CSBMs may offer modest, low-risk means of opening formerly closed relationships and of sustaining dialogue against the many irritations and (sometimes petty) disputes that mar progress on the path toward deeper cooperation. At the same time, efforts have been needed to ensure that CSBMs themselves did not fall prey to the vagaries of evolving and occasionally contentious relationships.

Institutional means of reviewing implementation and resolving disputes—insulated from the heat of public rhetoric—have been a feature of most successful confidence building efforts. In similar vein, successful confidence building has often been embedded in, and kept pace with, a larger process of political, economic, and cultural accommodation. Addressing military measures in parallel with economic development and scientific exchange, for example, may strengthen overall relationships, as long as setbacks in one sphere do not unnecessarily constrain initiatives in another.

Finally, the record suggests that CSBMs cannot be imposed from outside. Regions may borrow profitably from others' experience, but CSBMs must be in tune with the underlying political, economic, and cultural dynamics of individual regions. Regional ownership of proposed measures is a sine qua non of success.

A Survey of CSBMs by Category

Although all regions have addressed similar types of CSBMs, each has done so to different degrees and in different combinations. Communication and risk reduction measures have been most prominent in the Middle East and between the United States and the Soviet Union. Information exchange and notification and constraint of ground force operations have dominated in Europe and, in less ambitious forms, South Asia. Maritime measures—principally incidents at sea agreements—have figured widely in Russian bilateral initiatives with the United States and selected Western and, more recently, Pacific naval nations. Regional experience with different categories of CSBMs has varied as widely as the nations themselves. The implementation record nevertheless suggests some general lessons with regard to different types of measures.

Declaratory Measures

Declaratory measures—general statements of intent or principle—have ranged from the 1928 Briand-Kellogg Pact renouncing war to the 1971 Indo-Pakistani Simla Accord renouncing the use of force to resolve outstanding disputes. They have described general principles to guide relations, as in the CSCE Final Act, and they have expressed national commitments to unilateral action, for example, the pledge to improve national safeguards against unauthorized nuclear launch (included in the 1971 U.S.-Soviet Agreement on Measures to Reduce the Risk of Outbreak of Nuclear War).

This experience suggests that declaratory measures may be useful when they are used to resolve long-standing points of contention (e.g., acceptance of disputed borders) or to enunciate common principles against which to measure conduct. Experience also suggests, however, that declaratory measures are most beneficial when they carefully commit nations to specific undertakings, often in conjunction with more formal agreements or implementation measures.

Transparency Measures

A second general category of CSBMs, transparency measures, encompasses information exchange, communication, notification, and observation and inspection measures.

Information Exchange. Information measures cover a range of activity from military-to-military contacts to arms registries and detailed exercise calendar or data exchanges. Begun in

Europe as early as 1946–1947 with the introduction of U.S.-Soviet military liaison missions in Germany, information measures have been applied in progressively broader fashion to the European CSCE area through the 1986 Stockholm Conference on Confidence- and Security-Building Measures and Disarmament in Europe (CDE) Agreement and the 1990 and 1992 Vienna documents.

Such measures also have figured in Sino-Indian confidence building efforts, via agreements to exchange defense education and strategic studies institute personnel. With regard to nuclear facilities, the exchange of information on civilian programs was an important feature of the 1990 Joint Declaration on Nuclear Policy concluded between Argentina and Brazil.

Historically, some types of information measures (for example, military-to-military exchanges of students and staff officers) have occurred outside formal CSBM negotiations, early in a process of developing rapprochement. Other, more ambitious measures, including detailed data and calendar exchanges, have emerged as the result of sometimes lengthy negotiations, frequently fraught with disputes over the type and extent of data to be shared. The difficulty states experience in overcoming habits of secrecy in regard to military matters often creates barriers to openness that are broken down only after significant progress has been made in developing relations, suggesting to some that meaningful information exchanges follow rather than precede confidence building.

Such views, however, tend to underestimate the positive impact of even limited exchanges and contacts on developing patterns of routine cooperation and gaining acceptance of the idea that information on military forces and activities is a legitimate topic of concern for neighboring states. To be most effective in promoting such outlooks, however, information measures should not overreach the political willingness of states to share military data, lest they become an area of contention rather than cooperation.

Communication.   Communication measures address a range of crisis management and communication mechanisms, including hotlines, Conflict Prevention Centers (CPCs), and multilateral communication networks, as well as obligatory consultations on unusual or dangerous activities. Frequently appearing early in a process of conflict disengagement, communication measures have been negotiated in virtually every case of

confidence building reviewed for this chapter, including U.S.-
Soviet initiatives (1963 hotline and successor agreements), European CSBM negotiations (1990 multilateral communications network), South Asian disengagement efforts (Indo-Pakistani and
Sino-Indian hotlines and flag meetings), and, most recently, the
Middle East peace process (multilateral communications network).

The creation of direct communications channels is an important first step in fostering a more predictable, less crisis-prone
environment—particularly when contacts among adversaries
have been limited. As relationships mature, these networks may
be overtaken by a multiplying array of routine communications.
Nevertheless, experience under the extensive range of bilateral
and multilateral CSBM regimes featuring communications
arrangements suggests that such measures have virtually universal application across regions with very different geopolitical
characters.

Notification Measures.   Measures requiring the notification
of military activities from missile launches to ground force
maneuvers have figured widely in bilateral and multilateral
CSBM regimes from the 1971 U.S.-Soviet Agreement on Measures to Reduce the Risk of Outbreak of Nuclear War and the
1975 Helsinki Final Act to more recent Indo-Pakistani (1991),
Sino-Indian (1988–1993), and Sino-Russian (1993) agreements.
Typically applied to notification of ground force maneuvers,
these CSBMs have enjoyed mixed success. Although implemented faithfully in Europe, notification has been spotty
between India and Pakistan, reflecting continuing tension in the
relationship, the lack of an institutional mechanism for effective
follow-through, and (perhaps most important) the indifferent
attitudes of both governments to measures adopted under perceived pressure from outside.

    Unlike communication and information measures, which
appear to be universally applicable, notification measures must
be tailored to the specific forces and regions to which they will
apply. In this they take on some of the characteristics of technical
arms control. Notification thresholds must be carefully negotiated to ensure comparable treatment of forces with different military structures and exercise practice. Pre-notification windows
must be set with a view to the de facto constraints such measures
may imply, particularly for air and naval forces. In this regard,
nations have tended to resist notifying the movement of air and

naval units to avoid limiting their inherent flexibility and mobility. As a result, these measures may be less suitable for maritime environments where such forces predominate.

Observation and Inspection.   These measures include invitation of observers to military exercises and maneuvers, surveillance regimes and control zones, exercise or facility inspections, "Open Skies" aerial monitoring, and sensors and early warning stations. They may be applied unilaterally (e.g., seismic monitoring of nuclear tests), bilaterally, or multilaterally, and they may be carried out either by third parties or by the signatories themselves. Inspections may be routine or "challenge" and are typically intended to aid in verification efforts.

Historically, observation measures have figured prominently in UN (and other) peacekeeping and force separation agreements (e.g., in the Middle East, Cyprus, and India and Pakistan). In Europe, observation requirements, voluntary in the CSCE Final Act, have become progressively mandatory as successive agreements (1986, 1990, 1992) have unfolded. In the Middle East, third-party surveillance and monitoring of Arab-Israeli disengagement has been the norm. Observation and inspection measures have not featured in the Sino-Indian or Sino-Russian CSBM agreements.

These measures vary in scope and degree of intrusiveness, spanning the spectrum from voluntary invitation of observers to only large-scale exercises (CSCE Final Act) to detailed challenge inspections of suspect or sensitive facilities, possibly including nuclear, biological, or chemical infrastructure. At the latter extreme, inspection CSBMs differ little from inspection regimes associated with arms limitation accords, although in CSBM agreements, these measures tend to target military activities in contrast to force levels. Given the scope of observation and inspection measures, it is not surprising that they have played a role at virtually all stages of confidence building from the very early to the very advanced.

Surveillance CSBMs have been used in various ways, from force disengagement monitoring to non-military cooperation on ocean resources surveillance. This latter type of surveillance regime has been particularly common in the Asia Pacific, where it has included both multilateral (e.g., fisheries surveillance cooperation by the South Pacific Forum) and bilateral (e.g., Australia-Indonesia Timor Gap surveillance and Malaysia-Indonesia pollution monitoring) measures.[10]

Constraint CSBMs

Constraint CSBMs encompass risk reduction measures and exclusion/separation zones, as well as implicit or explicit limits on military personnel, equipment, and operational activities. Constraint CSBMs have more significant military impact than transparency measures and, as with their near cousin, formal treaty arms control, can be difficult to negotiate and verify.

Risk Reduction Measures. Exemplified by U.S.-Soviet Incidents at Sea and Dangerous Military Activity Agreements, risk reduction agreements are designed to prohibit or contain the consequences of inherently dangerous or inadvertent military activities, often by articulating codes of conduct for military forces, or by mandating crisis consultation and communication. Because they tend to address the consequences of mutually undesirable activities without unduly constraining operational forces, risk reduction measures have figured prominently early in the process of political and diplomatic rapprochement, often before political relations have been fully normalized. Periodic working level meetings designed to review compliance and resolve disputes have contributed to a record of successful implementation.

Although risk reduction measures have generally been implemented only in regard to military activity, the concept could be adapted to address risks at the intersection of military and economic interests. For example, such measures could define rules of conduct precluding military interference with commercial shipping, oil rig resupply, and so on. They could also be adapted to prescribe common security approaches and military roles with respect to non-state actors engaged in piracy or drug smuggling.

Constraint Measures. Constraints on personnel, equipment, and operational activities have tended to prohibit military operations that have not been properly forecast or notified, or that take place within certain exclusion or separation zones. Such measures have been most common in Europe, beginning with the 1986 CDE agreement, which tied ground force exercises to a predetermined schedule, and in the Middle East, where the Sinai and Golan disengagement agreements included constraining measures. Nuclear-free zones (and potentially other exclusionary zones) and nuclear testing restraints could also qualify as significant examples of constraint measures.

Constraining measures come closest of all CSBMs to technical arms control and thus pose challenges for negotiation and verification. Like notification, but to an even greater degree, constraining measures require significant tailoring to the force structure and practices of the region in which they are applied. Among constraint measures, nuclear-free zones (along the lines of the Tlatelolco and Rarotonga agreements) require perhaps the least technical preparation to negotiate and implement and, in regions where nuclear infrastructures are not entrenched, may serve as a point of entry for efforts to constrain military force. Other zones free of weapons of mass destruction are also theoretically possible, although to some degree already addressed in global nonproliferation efforts.

General Observations

What general observations does this survey of the implementation experience of different CSBMs suggest? First, it appears that some types of measures (information, communication, and risk reduction initiatives, for example) may be essentially universal in their applicability, while others (e.g., notification and constraint measures) require extensive tailoring to the force structures and regions in which they will be implemented. Operational constraints designed to limit opportunities for surprise attacks, for example, have little use in regions where defensive force structures offer limited prospect of such attacks.

Second, measures that overreach the political willingness of states to implement them can become sources of contention rather than accommodation and should be avoided. This suggests an implicit sequencing for confidence building activities that moves from lesser to greater degrees of intrusiveness and that keeps pace with the level of political rapprochement present in particular regions. Again, communication and risk reduction activities may prove easier to implement at earlier stages of accommodation than certain types of information, notification, or constraining measures.

Finally, some measures, particularly ones that are less constraining or intrusive, will be easier to negotiate and require less technical experience of arms control than initiatives (notification and constraining measures primarily) requiring detailed definition of thresholds or verification regimes. Absent sufficient technical and political preparation, such measures may tend to become bogged down in lengthy, perhaps unproductive negotiations.

Ultimately, the content of confidence building efforts may be less important than the process in instilling habits of cooperation that, over time, may result in greater understanding and increased levels of trust. This suggests that states should embark on confidence building without fixed notions of the measures most likely to contribute to enhanced security and without a detailed blueprint for negotiation. Preferred measures, instead, are those relevant initiatives with the best prospect of being negotiated and implemented. In regard to the Asia Pacific, accordingly, there should be a preference for measures that address the specific security problems of the region, taking into account its unique geostrategic character; that are relevant to the stage of political accommodation prevailing among regional states; that are consistent with regional strategic culture; and that build on the existing historical and institutional experience of the region.

Asia Pacific CSBM experience may be more extensive than commonly perceived. Existing regional initiatives include the bilateral regimes described earlier between India and Pakistan, India and China, China and Russia, and Russia and Japan, as well as the only partially successful efforts on the Korean peninsula. CSBM-type cooperation also occurs within Southeast Asia, centered around such ASEAN-sponsored initiatives as the publication of annual defense white papers, frequent military-to-military contacts, and bilateral and multilateral surveillance cooperation (in the Timor Gap and the Strait of Malacca). The "unofficial" Indonesian-sponsored dialogue on the South China Sea and Spratly Islands disputes provides another prospective confidence building endeavor.

Conclusion

Efforts to identify possible CSBMs for the Asia Pacific will confront several practical questions: What is the geostrategic focus for implementing CSBMs in Asia and how should subregional variations in the sources of tension, strategic dilemmas, and geographic setting be handled? How should confidence building efforts reconcile traditionally narrow interpretations of CSBMs as measures addressing military activity with the more expansive view of security (i.e., encompassing political, economic, and social dimensions) accepted in the region? How should the process of developing and implementing CSBMs take account of the more informal, less routinized styles of decision making inherent in much Asian diplomatic practice? What does the historical and institutional experience of the region suggest about the most fruitful directions for development of CSBMs? What kind of distinction, if any, should be drawn between CSBMs and joint or cooperative defense planning? Finally, how should regional initiatives relate to global regimes? Is there a role for regional nuclear, biological, chemical, and missile nonproliferation efforts, or will international regimes suffice?

This chapter is not intended to provide definitive answers to such questions nor to offer a menu of detailed initiatives. The review of past CSBM experience suggests, however, several general conclusions of relevance to Asia.

First, confidence building can be most successfully pursued as a step-by-step process focusing in the early stages on relatively modest, simple-to-negotiate initiatives that do not overreach the level of political accommodation among participating states. Such efforts can build toward more ambitious and progressively more intrusive measures at later stages but, as suggested earlier, should begin without preconceived ideas as to direction or timing.

Second, given the diverse geostrategic character of the region, confidence building in the Asia Pacific may be approached most usefully as a two- or three-tier process. Regionwide, attention can be given to risk reduction, communication, or information measures that are more universal in scope and less in need of tailoring to address specific geopolitical and military concerns. Subregionally, measures oriented more directly to the unique geographic and strategic character of the area can be implemented on either a bilateral or multilateral basis.

Third, while focusing on the military aspects of security, confidence building in Asia can be tailored to address the preconditions of political, economic, and social stability. For example, surveillance measures may give preference to protection of commercial shipping, fishing, or resource interests. Ground rules requiring self-restraint or transparency in military procurement can discourage diversion of resources from social and economic goals. Other "rules of the road" might preclude military interference with economic or commercial activity, particularly in disputed areas. Although CSBMs may focus narrowly on military security, they can still be embedded in a larger security framework encompassing political, economic, environmental, and cultural measures. Such initiatives could be pursued through a variety of diplomatic and institutional mechanisms related directly or indirectly to CSBMs. Preserving the distinction between CSBMs and other means of promoting regional stability, however, can help to ensure continued emphasis on concrete initiatives with measurable results. For similar reasons, it may also be desirable to preserve the emphasis on CSBMs as measures short of joint defense planning. A preference can be shown, however, for measures that set the stage for greater positive cooperation. Such initiatives might include joint surveillance arrangements and sharing of methodologies for defense planning, among other measures.

Fourth, as in the Middle East, limited experience with arms control in Asia suggests the need for educational efforts designed to enhance regional awareness of proposed CSBM initiatives. Unlike the Middle East, however, Asia is ill-suited to third-party mentoring efforts. In this regard, the second track process represented by the Council for Security Cooperation in the Asia Pacific (CSCAP) provides a forum for education and exploration that is more consistent with the less formalized strategic culture of the region. Other aspects of regional culture may argue for acceptance of the rule of consensus to guide CSBM deliberations; tolerance for evolving solutions; and acceptance of less structured, more multifaceted efforts in which bilateral and multilateral, regional, and subregional confidence building initiatives build cooperatively, if not chaotically, toward deeper relationships.[11]

Finally, there may be little benefit to regional mechanisms that merely duplicate international nonproliferation or arms transparency measures. This does not, however, argue that little can be done to strengthen regional nonproliferation efforts. Current regional participation in a series of global regimes, from the Nuclear Non-Proliferation Treaty (NPT) to the UN Register of Conventional Arms, is uneven or incomplete. Moreover, much could be done to develop regional initiatives that go beyond global commitments. Such measures might include a regional arms registry with more detailed reporting requirements than possible at the UN, regional nuclear or missile exclusion zones or bans, regional efforts at transparency in the biological field, or other information exchange provisions.

How important will confidence building measures be to the enhancement of security and cooperation in the Asia Pacific? Perhaps the greatest challenge to such measures lies, paradoxically, in the potential success of less structured approaches to regional security. With regional stability troubled more by latent than by active threats, particularly in Southeast Asia, greater confidence about the regional security environment could lessen the current momentum behind confidence building efforts. Moreover, although the need for CSBMs in Northeast Asia is likely to remain apparent, the preconditions for meaningful cooperation in that region as yet remain unfulfilled.

Notes

1. "Japan's Views Concerning the ASEAN Regional Forum (ARF)" (unpublished and undated paper by the Japanese Ministry of Foreign Affairs).

2. Cathleen S. Fisher, "The Preconditions of Confidence-Building: Lessons from the European Experience," in Michael Krepon et al., eds., *A Handbook of Confidence-Building Measures for Regional Security* (Washington, D.C.: Henry L. Stimson Center, September 1993), 31.

3. The terms by which confidence building measures (CBMs) or confidence and security building measures (CSBMs) have been known are also many and varied. First used in the mid-1950s in connection with U.S. and Soviet open skies and ground post control proposals at the UN, the term "confidence building measures" was later adopted to refer to the modest, politically binding, largely voluntary provisions on exercise notification and observation in the 1975 Helsinki Final Act of the Conference on Security and Cooperation in Europe (CSCE). The term "confidence- and security-building measures" (CSBMs) was introduced at the 1981–1983 CSCE Review Conference in Madrid by the neutral and nonaligned European nations to denote measures that were more "militarily significant, politically binding and verifiable" than earlier measures. Still earlier, Western delegations to the 1975–1986 Mutual and Balanced Force Reduction (MBFR) negotiations had proposed CSBM-type initiatives as "associated measures" to promote verification of conventional force limitations. The 1989–1992 Conventional Armed Forces in Europe (CFE) talks resurrected these measures as "stabilizing measures" designed to enhance verification. Finally, in an effort to establish a (more diverse, multipolar) Asian identity, new terms for CBMs in the Asia Pacific were used by some participants in the ASEAN Regional Forum (ARF) in Bangkok in July 1994—with the Japanese suggesting "Mutual Reassurance Measures (MRMs)" and the Australians suggesting "Trust-Building Measures (TBMs)." For the purposes of this chapter, CBMs and CSBMs are considered to be synonymous. For continuity purposes, the term "CSBMs" will be employed.

4. Desmond Ball, "The Most Promising CSBMs for the Asia/Pacific Region" (Paper prepared for an international conference on "The Asia-Pacific Region: Links between Economic and Security Relations," organized

by the Institute on Global Conflict and Cooperation, University of San Diego, May 13–15, 1993. It is interesting to note that the former Soviet Union and Warsaw Pact states also supported a more expansive view of what constitutes a CBM during CSCE negotiations. For these states, however, the concern appeared less to find a formulation compatible with the unique geopolitical character of their region than to avoid militarily concrete commitments limiting freedom of action.

5.   Johan Holst and Karen Alette Melander, "European Security and Confidence-Building Measures," *Survival* 19, no. 4 (July/August 1977): 146–154.

6.   They are implemented, however, as politically binding agreements.

7.   These included the 1971 Agreement to Reduce the Risks of Nuclear War, the 1972 Incidents at Sea Agreement, and the 1987 Nuclear Risk Reduction Centers and 1989 Dangerous Military Activities Agreements.

8.   U.S. Arms Control and Disarmament Agency, "Press Release of the Organization of American States (OAS) Governmental Experts Meeting on Confidence- and Security-Building Measures (CSBMs)," March 15–18, 1994, Buenos Aires, Argentina, April 12, 1994.

9.   "Detente is leading to India-China War Games," *International Herald Tribune*, December 17–18, 1994, p. 7.

10.   Dick Sherwood, "The Australian Experience with Maritime Cooperation" (Paper delivered to the Antalya Round of the MEPP Multilateral Working Group on Arms Control and Regional Security, Antalya, Turkey, March 21, 1994), p. 4.

11.   Ball, "The Most Promising CSBMs for the Asia/Pacific Region," 6–21.

6

Confidence Building in the Asia Pacific Region: Prospects and Problems

Margaret (Peggy) Mason

This chapter focuses first on defining the term "confidence building measures" and then turns to the "real lessons" of the European experience with the Conference on Security and Cooperation in Europe (CSCE). Next it considers the regional role of the United Nations (UN), particularly the Kathmandu process, in facilitating the process of confidence building in the Asian Pacific region. Finally, it relates both processes (confidence building per se and the UN's facilitation role) to the broader institution building process of which these two are fundamental parts. This will entail a brief consideration of some of the chief obstacles to the further development of global norms in the security domain, as well as of suggestions for a possible way ahead.

What Exactly Are Confidence Building Measures?

In turning anew to the vexing question of the definition of confidence building measures,[1] I was reminded of an article written in early 1990 by a well-known Canadian journalist on the occasion of the relaunching of the old Eisenhower idea for an "Open Skies" agreement covering all of Europe and North America. According to this deceptively simple scheme, individual states of the North Atlantic Treaty Organization (NATO) and the Warsaw Treaty Organization would be allowed to overfly states of the other group, on short notice, using unarmed observation-type aircraft.[2] After comparing arms controllers to Dale Carnegie instructors (because of their apparent "fixation" on confidence building),[3] the journalist went on to say that the phrase "confidence building" seemed to be like a mantra for arms control experts that, if chanted often enough, would take on "magical, though undefined" properties.

It may indeed be true that arms controllers—especially in the heady days immediately before and after the fall of the Berlin

Wall—ascribed to the CSCE process an almost mystical capability that later events in Yugoslavia irrefutably demonstrated that the process simply did not have. On the other hand, for anyone who has actually experienced the implementation of concrete transparency measures, it seems indisputable that the process is, indeed, greater than the sum of its parts.

Thus, while the expressions "confidence building measures" (CBMs) and "confidence and security building measures" (CSBMs) have been current in the context of arms control discussions—especially in the European context—since the early 1970s, the *concept* represented by those expressions remains nebulous.[4]

Confidence building is most frequently seen as a process of *communication* between governments concerning security-related matters. A second common element is that of *improving trust* or, conversely, eliminating mistrust and uncertainty. A third theme relates to arms control and disarmament. Disarmament is an incremental process, with CSBMs often linked to the early stages of that process. And, closely tied to these processes, particularly those likely to alter security arrangements, is the need to verify compliance. Verification itself is now looked at as *part* of the confidence building process.[5]

Most important, however, is the understanding that confidence building, if it is to be successful, must be treated as a process and not just a collection of individual measures or procedures intended to foster "transparency and predictability." CSBMs can help replace the subjective threat perception with objectively verifiable facts. Although there will necessarily be limits on the extent of the transparency, the key is not to prejudge the process. To encourage participation, it must be clearly understood that agreement on the first level of transparency (for example, observation of routine military exercises) does not commit the participants to any further steps. At the same time, it is vital not to "short-circuit" the process by ruling out potential future steps just because they are clearly premature in the initial stages.[6]

The Real Lessons from the European Experience

Confidence building must be viewed as a process, and not just a series of on-off measures, if its true potential for replacing confrontational patterns of interaction with cooperative ones is to be achieved. How then does it become a dynamic process? The extensive European experience of confidence building through the CSCE process suggests that confidence building measures simply cannot work to build confidence in the absence of a political decision to attempt to fundamentally alter the current (negative) security relationship between the relevant parties.[7] There must be some deliberate desire to move, however slowly, from misunderstanding and suspicion to mutual reassurance and, from there, toward active cooperation. Once this basic political decision is made, confidence building measures are the tools to help start to achieve this new security relationship and the interaction between the process of confidence building and the overall state of the political/security relationship becomes a mutually reinforcing one.

It is precisely this lack of genuine high-level commitment that explains why the fairly extensive series of CSBMs instituted between India and Pakistan—although mainly useful in and of themselves—have nonetheless failed to make any real dent in the fundamentally hostile security relationship between the two countries. In short, no "living process" has been engendered. One could go further and argue that, in some cases, the attempt to implement particular confidence building measures in isolation actually reinforced, rather than helped to overcome, existing suspicions.[8]

The second relevant lesson from Europe is that CSBMs are initial steps only. They lay a foundation, rather than substituting, for concrete conflict prevention and resolution mechanisms. Even CSBMs broadly defined to include transparency measures in relation to the verification of compliance with arms limitation and disarmament agreements are not sufficient. Arms control is not an end in itself. Neither are transparency measures. Although both are indispensable to a fully functioning cooperative security structure, they basically address certain symptoms of conflict, rather than underlying causes.

From this perspective, it is true that people, not guns, make war. Nonetheless, the quantity and quality of weapons can enormously complicate the search for solutions to the underlying security problems that triggered the arms buildup in the first place. It follows that, along with continued attention to arms control and disarmament, efforts should increasingly be devoted to the development of specific mechanisms for resolving the myriad disputes that currently exist between and among states. To put this another way, if it is such a tricky business to reach agreement on basic transparency measures—and efforts in the Asia Pacific region over the last five years would suggest that it is—why should it be any easier to develop functioning mechanisms for the peaceful resolution of disputes?[9]

The Europeans have surely learned this lesson the hard way. The CSCE process began in the early 1970s. It took until the end of 1986 to achieve agreement among the 35 participants on the notification, observation, and inspection of certain routine military exercises in order to provide verified assurances that the activities in question were, in fact, routine and, therefore, non-threatening.[10] In March 1989, in conjunction with the launching of the conventional force reduction talks among the 23 members of NATO and the Warsaw Treaty Organization, a new negotiation began in Vienna among the 35 CSCE participants, with the aim of further expanding the "system" of CSBMs in Europe.[11] With the fall of the Berlin Wall and the Vienna CSCE Summit in late 1990, European leaders declared that they had developed the "blueprint for the new security architecture of Europe."

The level of rhetoric and the sheer euphoria of participants in a process (which was suddenly on fast forward) tended to obscure the actual state of development of the CSCE to that point. Far from constituting a relatively mature process in the context of European security building, it was little more than a series of conferences with one concrete transparency agreement to its credit. In short, it represented a rather fragile international mechanism in the earliest stages of implementation.

One example should suffice. Part of the new European security architecture elaborated in the Vienna Document was a Conflict Prevention Center (CPC)—at least this is what it was called. Yet, despite the best efforts of a few,[12] it was not given a mandate to elaborate conflict prevention and resolution mechanisms. It was explicitly confined, instead, to developing yet more confidence building measures.

It is impossible to say whether a fully functioning CPC with procedures for conciliation, mediation, and arbitration could have prevented the conflict in Yugoslavia; we shall never know. The point is that, once the fire begins to smolder, smoke detectors are of little value if the fire engine has not yet been built.

On the other hand, as essential as a fully functioning dispute resolution mechanism is, it cannot be created in the absence of some level of confidence and trust. The initial, painstaking steps to build confidence through greater openness and predictability in military matters cannot be skipped over. This is third lesson from Europe. A dynamic confidence building regime is the product of sustained efforts over time. The process must ripen to the point at which the participants are ready to supplement transparency measures with arms limitation obligations and with agreed procedures for the peaceful resolution of disputes.[13] With the best will in the world, this is a slow process. It is imperative that Asia Pacific states make a more concerted effort to move forward while the conditions are so propitious.

The Regional Role of the United Nations

Progress may be facilitated if better account is taken of developments at the global level that have effectively "internationalized" certain broad principles in relation to confidence building and openness in military matters.

In 1988, the United Nations Disarmament Commission (UNDC), a deliberative body comprising all member states of the UN, reached agreement on "guidelines for appropriate types of confidence-building measures and for the implementation of such measures on a global or regional level."[14] In 1992, the Commission reached agreement on guidelines and recommendations in relation to "Oneness in Military Matters" (OIMM) and, in 1993, an agreement was finalized on "regional approaches" to arms limitation and disarmament. The latter agreement included a specific section on "confidence- and security-building measures" (section III) as well as an appendix containing an "illustrative List of confidence- and security-building measures."

The process of negotiating each of these agreements was an arduous and lengthy one. At the onset of the OIMM negotiation in 1990, the representative of the People's Republic of China stated forthrightly that his country did not agree with openness in military matters. Nonetheless, by the end of the three-year negotiation, China had joined the consensus in respect of this "political commitment."[15]

Yet, in the Senior Officials Meeting to prepare for the first ministerial session of the ASEAN Regional Forum (ARF), China (among others) opposed, as premature, the establishment of a Working Group to elaborate CSBMs. This "disconnect" between the disarmament apparatus of the foreign ministry and the rest of the state's security machinery is one of the many unfortunate legacies of the cold war. For almost 50 years, the primary role of arms control and disarmament was to manage East-West tension. In the global deliberative bodies, this translated into "the many" exhorting "the few" to stop building, and start reducing the number of, nuclear weapons. This, in turn, meant that many countries were negotiating texts in the global deliberative bodies without attention to the regional or subregional context (even where the documents specifically provided for such application).

Now that the post-cold war focus has turned quite specifically to regional and subregional problems, the point is that we are not beginning with a blank slate. Concepts have been "worked through"—however disingenuously by some at the global level—and, therefore, reflect a genuine effort to separate principles of general application from region-specific measures that might not "travel" well to other geographic locations.

This brings us to a discussion of the UN-sponsored regional security dialogue mechanism, known informally as the Kathmandu process. Begun in 1989, an annual seminar has been held in Kathmandu, co-hosted by the New York-based UN Centre for Disarmament Affairs (CDA) and by the Kathmandu-based UN Regional Centre for Peace and Disarmament,[16] with the avowed purpose of promoting and facilitating a broad-ranging regional security dialogue. Participants are a combination of government officials (mainly, but not exclusively, disarmament ambassadors) and nongovernmental experts, all invited to attend in their "personal" capacity. In short, the UN-sponsored process would appear to be very much like other track two dialogue channels in the Asia Pacific, more than 40 of which were catalogued by Paul Evans in June 1994.[17]

However, as I have frequently said elsewhere,[18] the UN-sponsored process is unique because it alone brings with it the framework of norms and principles developed at the global level. In essence, its "regional role" is to promote dialogue as the first step to security cooperation in a manner that helps ensure a complementary and mutually reinforcing interaction between the global and regional levels. The presence of the UN not only helps legitimate the process of regional security cooperation but also provides important guidance on the agenda to be pursued. In this regard, it is worth noting that the words "confidence building" have appeared in the title of every Kathmandu Seminar held since its inception.[19]

Despite its considerable potential, the Kathmandu process faces considerable difficulties. Only the salary of the director is paid out of the regular UN budget. All other activities depend on voluntary "pledges" from member states, private foundations, and in some cases, even municipal governments.[20] Equally problematic is the continuing segregation of disarmament issues and disarmament expertise from the broader security dialogue process that is now under way.[21] The Kathmandu process, for example, has tended to attract mainly officials who are responsible for multilateral disarmament issues, despite efforts to include strategic analysts and defense planners. Conversely, the main nongovernmental dialogues (such as the annual Asia Pacific Roundtable) have relatively few "disarmers" in proportion to the security analysts and, indeed, in relation to "regional dialoguers" in general. Significantly at the UN-sponsored meeting in Hiroshima in May 1994,[22] disarmament experts and regional specialists were in roughly equal proportions and discovered, perhaps not unsurprisingly, that they had some difficulty in understanding each other!

The regional role in the UN as described in this chapter is being impeded by a far more insidious problem than inadequate financing or excessive compartmentalization of expertise. Increasingly, the normative framework the UN brings to the regional table is being undermined.

The Global Normative Framework

The Nuclear Non-Proliferation Treaty

To illustrate this disheartening thesis, let us briefly consider the most elaborated and codified of the global arms control norms, the nuclear nonproliferation regime at the heart of which lies the Nuclear Non-Proliferation Treaty (NPT) and its concomitant system of international safeguards under the auspices of the International Atomic Energy Agency (IAEA). The NPT has the largest and most comprehensive membership of any arms control treaty in existence today.[23] It also has the most comprehensive system of verification currently in operation.[24]

On January 31, 1992, in the wake of the Persian Gulf War revelations of massive conventional and unconventional arms buildups in Iraq, the UN Security Council, at its first-ever summit meeting, declared that the proliferation of weapons of mass destruction was a "threat to international peace and security." This unanimous statement was potent evidence of the Council's determination to enforce the nuclear nonproliferation norm in accordance with its Charter-mandated "primary responsibility for the maintenance of international peace and security"(article 24).

Yet, despite this impressive veneer of international agreement, a mere scratching of the surface reveals that the nonproliferation norm is only skin-deep. With less than a year to go until a meeting to decide on the duration of the treaty's extension, the international community is moving inexorably toward a North/ South confrontation that, if it does not fatally imperil the treaty at the core of the global nonproliferation regime, will leave it legally in force, but with substantially weakened authority.

Almost all of the parties to the treaty from the developed world have called for the indefinite and unconditional extension of the NPT,[25] arguing that it is the linchpin of the international community's efforts to combat "horizontal" nuclear proliferation. These same countries have rejected as counterproductive any "negative linkage" between extension of the treaty and further progress on "vertical proliferation." Most of the Western *non*-nuclear weapon states, however, have called for "parallel progress" to further reduce the "vertical" proliferation of nuclear weapons, in accordance with article VI (the disarmament provisions) of the treaty.

In contrast, most nonaligned states parties have *not* committed themselves to indefinite extension, preferring some arrangement that makes extension conditional on further concrete progress toward nuclear disarmament. It is not so much that they minimize the steps already taken by the United States and Russia,[26] or the significance of the participation by all five nuclear weapon states in the Geneva negotiation to permanently ban nuclear explosive testing. Rather, they fear that, once the NPT is "safely" extended for an indefinite period, the five states will lose any further interest in pursuing an end to their nuclear "have" status. In short, the nonaligned states that are parties to the NPT fear that "indefinite and unconditional extension" of the treaty will come to mean an indefinite and unconditional extension of the privileges of the five—the very same five who are also the permanent members of the Security Council.[27]

The nonaligned states parties would like to see article VI of the treaty given due weight. In addition to substantial progress toward the conclusion of a comprehensive test ban treaty (CTBT), they would like to see the current unilateral declarations of the five replaced by one legally binding commitment not to use or threaten to use nuclear weapons against any non-nuclear weapon state. Some, like Egypt, are insisting that Security Council resolution 255 (1968)—which provides a "positive assurance" of aid to a state so threatened—be considerably strengthened.

Beyond the specifics is a desire that the nuclear weapon states somehow make more credible the commitment to eventual nuclear disarmament that the nonaligned (and many others) believe is embodied in the tortuous language of article VI (and the preamble to the treaty). They point to the Chemical Weapons Convention, which abolishes that particular category of weapons of mass destruction, as the appropriate model to apply now to nuclear weapons.

Calls for a specific timetable for nuclear disarmament would appear unrealistic in today's very uncertain international security environment, but Western nuclear weapon states should, at a minimum, be willing to contemplate a substantive review of the operation of the NPT over the last 25 years, including a frank discussion of the obstacles to, and the necessary preconditions for, eventually moving to nuclear disarmament. Thus far, the Western three (France, the United Kingdom, and the United States) have been adamant in their refusal to consider such a dialogue,[28] referring to the 1995 meeting as an "Extension Conference" only, while the nonaligned call it a "Review and Extension Conference." Caught in the middle, the UN Secretariat charged with technical preparations for the conference uses the "1995 Conference of the Parties to the Treaty on the Non-Proliferation of Nuclear Weapons."

And so, the dialogue of the deaf continues, with the North largely focusing on horizontal proliferation and the South on vertical. Against this background, if the circumstances surrounding the Security Council Summit Declaration are more closely examined, one finds that India, prior to allowing the "consensus" statement to go forward, made what might be called a preemptive interpretive disclaimer. In essence India said that its support for the declaration must be interpreted in light of its long-standing position against nuclear proliferation "in all its aspects" and in favor of a multilaterally negotiated, nondiscriminatory ban on nuclear weapons.[29]

Indian criticism of the NPT is as old as the treaty itself. What was new in January 1992 was the extent of the Indians' verbal acrobatics in their efforts to avoid appearing to flout the international community's determination to take effective action to stem further horizontal proliferation. Now, in November 1994, international solidarity has been so dissipated that India—a nonparty and bitter foe of the NPT—finds its views echoed by most of the nonaligned states parties to the treaty.

This rift within the nuclear nonproliferation regime is not only threatening the smooth extension of the NPT; it is also undermining international efforts to take effective action in the case of treaty noncompliance. The attitude of the nonaligned appears to be that those who selectively interpret the rules can be left to enforce them on their own. But effective enforcement requires a robust international norm. This, in turn, requires broad international support. Renegades must truly be isolated.

Take the case of North Korea. Whatever leverage the international community might have had in relation to this isolated and archaic regime was severely undercut by the lack of a united front. This is not to suggest that the nonaligned supported North Korean contravention of its treaty obligations; quite the contrary. Yet, despite their clear distaste for a nuclear-armed North Korea, they were unwilling to take more than token steps to admonish the regime. Indonesia, chair of the Non-Aligned Movement during this critical period—and clearly disquieted over the possible domino effect of a nuclear-armed Korean peninsula—chose inaction rather than be accused of siding with the North.

Nonaligned indifference to North Korea's flagrant violation of its NPT safeguards obligations, in turn, let China off the hook. Rather than exerting every effort to convince Pyongyang to come back into treaty compliance, China used its influence and the threat of its veto largely to prevent timely and concerted action by the IAEA Board of Governors and the UN Security Council.[30] China counseled dialogue and negotiation but, in the absence of the leverage only it could provide, this really meant bribing North Korea back into compliance. Even when this strategy was pursued in earnest by the United States, China only helped clinch the North Korean "buy-back-in" deal at the eleventh hour. China might well have taken a different approach if it had risked strong disapproval from the nonaligned for failing to do so.

The widening North-South split over the scope of the nonproliferation obligations codified in the NPT is the most urgent and pressing example of the need to reforge a consensus on the nuclear nonproliferation norm if it is to be effectively enforceable over the medium term.

The Missile Technology Control Regime

The second battleground over who determines the content of the nonproliferation standard is the territory of export controls and their associated supplier coordination mechanisms. Supplier arrangements rest initially on the premise that producers of sensitive technologies have both the inherent right, and the public duty, to seek to ensure that their exports do not contribute to the proliferation of weapons of mass destruction. In addition, suppliers also seek to justify their actions in relation to the fulfillment, where applicable, of codified obligations. To this end, they argue that effective implementation of the nonproliferation norm quite simply requires supplier coordination. They point out that harmonized arrangements that replace a plethora of potentially conflicting national approaches actually facilitate, rather than impede, trade in dual-use technologies for peaceful purposes.

Problems begin to arise, however, when the standard set by the supplier group is more rigorous than that codified multilaterally or, alternatively, when there is no multilateral standard.

The supplier cartel that is least related to a global mechanism is the Missile Technology Control Regime (MTCR), the agreement (originally among seven Western suppliers) to strictly control certain (mainly dual-use) technologies relevant to the development of ballistic missiles.[31] The MTCR is the proverbial red flag to a bull. It is the antithesis of multilateral agreement because of its exclusivity and its almost complete lack of transparency. Even prospective new members of the club complain that, once in, they may not receive the same level of information as the original seven. (This has been a persistent complaint of Russia, for example).

Despite the tenuous relationship between the MTCR and multilaterally negotiated obligations, the United States persists in describing it as a "multilateral, non-proliferation agreement." One can make the argument that any agreement with more than two parties is a multilateral one, but the term has come to mean an agreement that, at some state of its negotiation, has been opened to the international community at large. This is not the case now with the MTCR, nor has it ever been.

To attempt to put on the same footing, on the one hand, arrangements negotiated by a handful of Western suppliers and then unilaterally imposed on everyone else, and, on the other, treaties that have been negotiated and agreed to by the international community at large is to undermine the very notion of internationally codified norms.

Let me underscore that my argument is not intended to suggest that the MTCR is unnecessary. Suppliers cannot wait until global agreements are negotiated before they control their sensitive exports. Such interim measures actually permit and facilitate legitimate trade in the absence of comprehensive arrangements. The point is, however, that these are *not* global arrangements.

They are not multilaterally negotiated; to suggest otherwise is to reinforce the notion that what is meant by a "global norm" is really what the United States (and a few of its closest allies) want it to mean at a particular moment in time.[32]

This perception is reinforced by the apparent contempt of the Western three for the norm building efforts of the global deliberative bodies.[33] For example, the UN Disarmament Commission worked for four years to develop preliminary guidelines and principles in relation to the transfer for peaceful purposes of sensitive dual-use technologies. The initiative, originally conceived by Argentina and Brazil, subsequently became a joint effort by Brazil and Canada.[34] From the outset it was made clear that this effort was very much a preliminary first step, an effort to promote multilateral dialogue toward the eventual development of agreed guidelines between supplier and recipient. Brazil was at pains to point out that the aim of the exercise was neither to undermine existing ad hoc measures nor to lower standards, but rather to make them more effective by broadening and deepening their coverage through multilateral negotiations. The attitude of the Western three can best be characterized by their refusal to commit themselves to even the objective of multilateral guidelines.

The attitude of the South was also problematic, with game playing and unrealistic demands often superseding serious negotiating positions. Nonetheless, in the end, when the time to make a deal had almost run out, the nonaligned were ready to agree to a reasonable text while the United States, the United Kingdom, and France were not.

The unilateralism of major Western suppliers has driven even the most moderate nonaligned countries to support Iranian and Indian denunciations of all export controls that are not "multilaterally negotiated, non-discriminatory, universally accepted and acceptable." Taken literally, those requirements would give every country—including those patently determined to be irresponsible—a veto over the development of genuinely multilateral controls. It is important to note, however, that the bulk of the nonaligned are not, in fact, using the literal interpretation. The point at issue is not really whether every single country would have to agree before the standard was sufficiently internationalized, but rather the status of interim measures while the negotiation is taking place. Because of the refusal of major suppliers to seriously engage in even preliminary dialogue, the

Non-Aligned movement, at its last four summit meetings, has unanimously denounced all interim measures as illegitimate.

Recommendation and Conclusion

How can this escalating confrontation between developed and developing countries start to be defused? How can a process be undertaken that offers some realistic prospect for the development of guidelines for dual-use transfers that meet the basic requirements of both suppliers and recipients. (This question is all the more pressing as one considers the number of countries in the Asia Pacific region in transition from strictly importer status to one of "emerging supplier" as well.)

First and foremost, the cavalier attitude of the Western three to the norm building efforts that are the essence of the work of global deliberative bodies must be replaced by a more sophisticated appraisal of the appropriate balance between the prerogatives of the General Assembly and those of the Security Council. (Anecdotal evidence suggests that this lesson has already been learned by the U.S. Permanent Mission in New York, but responsibility for disarmament activities lies with the Geneva-based delegation.)

If the nonaligned are serious about more than exposing the hypocrisy of the Western great powers, there is much that they can also start to do at the regional and subregional levels where the negative reinforcement of the Western three's "unity" and European Union political coordination is simply not present. The "almost agreed" guidelines on the transfer of dual-use technologies can be examined in the context of a track two working group to see if there are useful elements upon which to agree.[35]

Similarly, the meaning of the words "excessive and destabilizing accumulations of conventional weapons" from the 1992 Security Council Summit Declaration can be considered in the context of ASEAN, the North Pacific, and the region as a whole. If Asia Pacific countries do not want a definition "imposed" on them from outside, serious and timely efforts must be undertaken to give content to this concept in a manner that duly reflects the particularities of this region.

In this regard, the Najib proposal for discussions on a regional register of conventional arms merits greater attention and support, not least from the Malaysian Foreign Ministry.[36] One complementary step would be for ASEAN governments to agree to implement in their subregion the CSCAP proposal for a Resource and Information Center on holdings and transfers of conventional armaments.[37]

Finally, it is essential that UN-sponsored activities develop much broader outreach into the defense and security communities of the countries in the region. Perhaps one approach might be for the UN to co-host, with interested governments, country-specific seminars targeted at defense planners and strategic analysts as well as disarmament experts. CSCAP should also consider conferring "observer" status on the UN Regional Center or its director, Tsutomu Ishiguri.

A final word about Chinese intentions. In chapter 2 of this volume Robert Manning concludes that

> China's pro forma participation in nascent security dialogues while impeding any serious attempts at preventive diplomacy, amid its continuing military modernization, suggests a strategy of calculated ambiguity designed to result in an outcome on Chinese terms.

I believe that China will continue to maximize its options for unilateral action unless and until (and only if) it is hemmed in by a genuine consensus involving at least a majority of the nonaligned countries with which China identifies. In practical terms this means that, if the ASEAN Regional Forum is to be anything more than a grandiose talk shop, care must be taken to avoid giving China a preemptive veto. ASEAN countries can always hide behind China if they wish. As the stalemate over the Spratly Islands would seem to suggest, however, it may now be in their interest to move cautiously in front of China and let Beijing decide whether or not to clearly be the spoiler or to more forthrightly embrace the new opportunities for mutual reassurance and cooperation in the Asia Pacific region.

Notes

1. See Peggy Mason, "Confidence- and Security-Building Measures for the Asia-Pacific Region," *Disarmament Topical Papers 7*, United Nations Publication, 1992, where I first tackled this issue in the context of the Asia Pacific region. For a definitive analysis of the evolution of confidence and security building measures in the CSCE context, see James Macintosh, *Confidence-(and Security-) Building Measures in the Arms Control Process: A Canadian Perspective* (Ottawa: Department of External Affairs, August 1985).

2.   The idea was denounced in 1955 by the Soviet Union as nothing short of "legalized espionage." At the opening of the conference in Ottawa in February 1990, Eduard Shevardnadze, then Soviet foreign minister, declared that an Open Skies Agreement would stand as a model for building a "global confidence system."

3.   Dale Carnegie is an American who popularized seminars on how to project confidence when engaged in public speaking, chairing a meeting, or otherwise interacting with the public.

4.   For the purposes of this paper, the two terms will be seen as interchangeable. CSBMs will be employed for continuity's sake.

5.   Behind this now banal statement, however, are at least 16 years of insistence by some that the two sets of concepts must be kept rigidly separate.

6.   Contrast this view with the insistence by some Australians (Paul Dibb, for example) that a clear distinction be made, ab initio, regarding the types of information that should and should not be the subject of CSBMs. In particular, Dibb argues that information on weapons holdings should *not* be included.

7.   The CSCE has three related, but distinct, "baskets" of issues: the human dimension, scientific and technical cooperation, and security concerns. The first CSBM agreement was negotiated at the 1986 Stockholm Conference, the security forum of the CSCE process.

8.   I have in mind the agreement not to attack each other's nuclear installations, which soon degenerated into a fight over the accuracy of the lists of sites that were exchanged. (This example also speaks to the need for *verified* CSBMs!)

9.   Such efforts are indeed taking place. The Indonesian-hosted (and Canadian-financed) series of workshops on the Spratly Islands is one important example of a "track two" process to this end. The point is that confidence building should be seen in relation to preventive diplomacy as a necessary precursor or at least concomitant activity.

10.   The cold war version of the CSCE encompassed all the countries of the European continent (except Albania), plus Canada and the United States.

11.   Note that, while Canada and the United States were full participants in the CSCE from the outset, the geographical focus was limited to Europe, including the then-Soviet Union "east of the Urals." The first confidence building regime to aim at all of Europe, all of the then Soviet Union, and North America (excluding Mexico) was the Open Skies negotiation, launched in Ottawa in February 1990.

12.   Canada and Germany in particular.

13.   Interestingly, the Association of Southeast Asian Nations (ASEAN), which has been described as a very successful confidence building mechanism, did begin to elaborate such procedures. The 1976 Treaty of Amity and Cooperation elaborates principles for interstate conduct and procedures for the peaceful resolution of disputes. This is a promising start. However, much remains to be done. See, for example, Muthiah Alagappa,

"Security in South-East Asia: Beyond a Zone of Peace, Freedom and Neutrality (ZOPFAN)," *Disarmament Topical Papers 6*, 1991, pp. 118–133.

14.   The General Assembly endorsed these guidelines by its resolution 43/78H on December 7, 1988.

15.   The UN Disarmament Commission works "by consensus"; an objection by any participant blocks agreement. Because the forum is "deliberative" and not a formal negotiating body, the agreement reached constitutes a "political commitment" rather than a legally binding treaty.

16.   The UNCDA comprises that part of the UN Secretariat in New York responsible for overseeing all UN-related arms control and disarmament activities. The term "based" is used somewhat loosely. The General Assembly resolution that authorized the establishment of the three regional centers specified their locations as Kathmandu for the Asia Pacific center, Lima for the center representing Latin America and the Caribbean, and Lomé for the African regional center. Because of inadequate financing and other problems, however, the Kathmandu Centre is actually directed out of New York with the only in situ activity being the annual seminar.

17.   Paul Evans, "Existing Regional Security Dialogues in Asia-Pacific," *Disarmament Topical Papers 20*, 1994, pp. 192–201. Evans defines track two channels as "blended" meetings, involving academics, journalists, and (generally), government officials, particularly from the Foreign Ministry, but also sometimes from defense ministries. In all cases, participants are invited in their "personal capacity."

18.   See, for example, my "Efforts to Promote Regional Security Dialogue and Cooperation in the North Pacific," *Disarmament Topical Papers 20*, pp. 69–70.

19.   Input from the region is having its effect on the UN process however. The seventh Kathmandu meeting, set for February 1995, is entitled "Openness, *Assurance of Security* and Disarmament" (emphasis added).

20.   When the General Assembly originally mandated the establishment of the three regional centers, many, if not most, Western member states were quite skeptical about their utility. With the demise of the cold war and the concomitant rise in the importance of regional approaches to peace and security, and given the UNCDA's deft handling of the limited resources at its disposal, the view of Western member states has generally changed quite dramatically. Japan, initially quite hostile to regional approaches, is now a major funder of Kathmandu activities. Unfortunately, the United States, the United Kingdom, and France still object to funding any of these activities out of the regular UN budget, insisting on continued reliance on voluntary pledges. Of the three, only France has made such voluntary pledges.

21.   This is no idle concern. A lack of adequate planning with respect to the arms control dimension of peace operations can directly contribute to the failure of the overall operation, Somalia being a tragic case in point.

22.   The Hiroshima Conference on "Transparency in Armaments, Regional Dialogue and Disarmament," took place on May 24–27, 1994.

23. All five declared nuclear weapon states are parties, as are 160 non-nuclear weapon states.

24. Once the Chemical Weapons Convention is in force and its verification agency, the Organization for the Prohibition of Chemical Weapons, is fully operational, this statement may need to be qualified.

25. Switzerland may be the exception.

26. Nonetheless, they frequently point out, as Jonathan Dean recently did, that implementation of all of the commitments made thus far would reduce operationally deployed U.S. and Russian strategic-range nuclear weapons to their levels when the NPT entered into force in the 1970s. See Jonathan Dean, "The Final Stage of Nuclear Arms Control," *The Washington Quarterly* 17, no. 4 (autumn 1994): 31–52.

27. This view is widely shared by the interested public in Western countries. Canada's former ambassador for disarmament, Douglas Roche, who has maintained close ties with Canadian and New York-based NGOs, has vigorously criticized the UN secretary general's support for indefinite and unconditional extension. (In my view, this criticism is misplaced. Boutros-Boutros Ghali has made it clear that further significant steps toward nuclear disarmament are also needed.)

28. China has frequently called for negotiations to abolish nuclear weapons, no doubt secure in the knowledge that its demands would go safely unheeded. In the meantime, on the basis that it lags far behind those states "with the largest military capabilities," China is continuing its nuclear weapons testing program.

29. India has long maintained that it will only accede to the NPT when the treaty's ban on nuclear weapons applies equally to all states.

30. Although China could not block a referral of the North Korean matter to the Security Council by the IAEA Board of Governors, its veto in the Council could nonetheless make that referral futile.

31. I say "least related" because, although there is no multilateral agreement banning ballistic missiles, a credible argument can be made that, insofar as the technology being controlled is related to delivery vehicles for weapons of mass destruction (and not conventionally armed missiles), the regime can legitimately be said to be "in furtherance" of a state party's nuclear nonproliferation obligations under the NPT.

32. I emphasize "at a moment in time" because the U.S. view of a particular obligation, even one that has the sanction of the UN Security Council, is all too dependent on the vagaries of domestic politics. The purported congressional "override" of the UN arms embargo on Bosnia speaks volumes on the American institutional blindness to the distinction between national interests and international processes.

33. The term "contempt" is not used lightly. It is based on the author's personal experience over five years in heading Canada's delegation to the global deliberative bodies.

34. Brazil is an emerging supplier while Canada was an original participant in the exclusive MTCR club.

35.   In this case, "almost agreed" means that *retention* of one sentence of one paragraph of one section was opposed by one country and its *deletion* objected to by three. Surely, there is something useful in the rest that is worth further examination.

36.   The idea first surfaced in a speech by the Malaysian minister of defense given in Darwin, Australia, in early 1992. It is well known that the Foreign Ministry has not been entirely enthusiastic about the progressive, high-profile steps on regional dialogue that have been taken by the dynamic minister of defense.

37.   CSCAP envisages a nongovernmental body with sufficient government backing to enable it to access the data it would be expected to compile.

7

Step-By-Step Confidence and Security Building for the Asian Region: A Chinese Perspective

Liu Huaqiu

The end of the cold war has terminated the confrontation between the two major military blocs but has not meant an end to all war and potential conflict. Tension, turbulence, even wars have emerged in some areas, as in Bosnia, Somalia, Haiti, and elsewhere. Although the situation in the Asian region is relatively stable, there are still many problems that bear on security in this region. For several years, the states in the region have begun to search for new measures to promote stability and cooperation with their neighbors. This makes the issue of confidence building measures (CBMs) and confidence and security building measures (CSBMs) all the more relevant as an element in the creation of an alternative to traditional approaches to national security and international peace in today's interdependent and interactive regional and global context.

Europe versus Asia

The European experience in the field of confidence building measures has been effective in promoting transparency, openness, and predictability in the military environment. It has helped to improve the political climate among states belonging to the two military blocs as well as neutral and non-aligned states. It contributed to a certain extent to the process that led to the signing of the Conventional Armed Forces in Europe and Strategic Arms Reduction Treaties and the unilateral reduction of theater nuclear weapons by the North Atlantic Treaty Organization and the Warsaw Pact.

Some believe that the measures and tools developed in Europe can easily be transferred to other regions and ask with the best of intentions why a "Conference on Security and Cooperation in Asia" (similar to the Conference on Security and Cooperation in Europe or CSCE) could not be developed to address security issues in Asia. This suggestion has not received a warm response from the majority of Asian states concerned. This is not to say that the European experience with CSBMs is not useful. On the contrary, Asian states can learn much from the European experience. The question is how to learn. Many states believe that what they learn must be adapted to the unique cultural, historic, political, and economic conditions of their region. Therefore, in approaching the issue of probable Asian CSBMs, it is necessary to go briefly into the differences between the situation in Asia and that in Europe.

First, Europe was divided into two major military blocs, which were diametrically opposed in tense confrontation. There is no clear bloc confrontation in Asia; the demarcation lines between friend and foe intersect and overlap, and they often change with the passage of time and the evolution of events. Attitudes among Asian states toward many international issues are complex.

Second, the Asian concept of security differs from that of the states in Europe. Europe was the scene of two world wars in which the people in Europe suffered seriously. The direct confrontation of the two military blocs made Europe a potential ground for another world war. Therefore, the primary security goal for the European states was to cut the armament levels of both sides and to terminate the protracted and serious military standoff in Europe. In approaching this goal, it was most imperative to build all kinds of confidence and security measures in order to prevent an accidental war.

As for the Asian region, with the exception of the former Soviet Union and Japan, most states were reduced to the status of colonies and semi-colonies in the past, were subject to invasion and plunder by alien forces, and were confronted with quite a few contradictions stirred up by the colonialists on territorial and border issues. For example, the Kashmir issue handed down by the British colonialists when they left the South Asian subcontinent has led to three wars between India and Pakistan. The MacMahon Line (which the British had illegally drawn) has been the root of border trouble between China and India. In addition, there are disputes over the four islands of the "Northern Territories" between Russia and Japan, the Sino-Russia border, and China's South Sea and its islands. Ethnic and religious contradictions also give rise to political turbulence in some states.

Asian CSBMs

As a result of this background, the traditional concept of security in the Asian region is mainly to prevent external intervention and invasion and to preserve national sovereignty and territorial integrity.[1] The situation in the Asian region is more complicated than the singular East-West confrontation that existed in Europe. We should not, therefore, mechanically copy the CSCE model of CSBMs. A pragmatic approach would begin by considering the specific conditions, the roots of conflict, and the potential sources of accommodation. Then we can craft a confidence and security building strategy appropriate to the region.

In view of the above-mentioned conditions, I favor an incremental approach. Actually, confidence building in Europe was also a step-by-step process. The measures agreed to by the CSCE member states were carefully developed through years of patient negotiations and refined following the experience of their earlier application.[2] Cathleen S. Fisher has divided confidence building in Europe into four phases:

Pre-CBMs:	Soviet-American agreements
First-generation CBMs:	Ground breakers (the Helsinki CBMs)
Second-generation CBMs:	Security-building measures (the Stockholm and Vienna Accords)
Third-generation CBMs:	Cooperative security measures

Fisher concluded, "if there is any broader lesson to be drawn from the European experience, it is the importance of modest expectations, patience, and an appreciation of small gains in trust."[3] The question is not whether CSBMs are relevant and applicable to other regions, but how much adaptation and creativity will be required in order to meet the unique confidence building needs of particular regions.

Many Western people regard CSBMs as a panacea. It seems that they have overestimated their initial role in European disarmament and arms control. The question to be posed is, have European CSBMs led to the present state of European disarmament? Or, has the logic of the process been quite a different one, in which CSBMs have proved to be a limited, initial step under precise circumstances, while in their further development the logic of CBMs has been overridden by more important factors of a different origin?

According to Alexei V. Zagorsky, the European process of disarmament was guided by two other concepts: the concept of non-offensive defense, elaborated mostly by European Social Democrats (primarily Scandinavian and German), and, later, the Soviet notion of sufficient defense, with each evolving closer to the other by the end of the 1980s.[4] In addition, the political changes in Central and Eastern Europe in 1989–1990 (and also the disintegration of the Soviet Union) should not be underestimated as providing the strongest push to radicalize the whole approach to European security.

Recommendations

It is quite evident that political will is to a great extent the basis for the institution of CSBMs. On the basis of the above-mentioned situation and assessments, I would make the following recommendations:

- Establish norms of state-to-state relations, to serve as guidelines to confidence and security building for the Asian region;

- Take an incremental approach;

- Promote denuclearization of the Korean peninsula;

- Work toward an agreement on no-first-use of nuclear weapons and promote the establishment of nuclear-weapon-free zones and zones of peace in the region;

- Extend the Missile Technology Control Regime (MTCR) into a treaty, like the Nuclear Non-Proliferation Treaty (NPT), in order to encourage more states to participate in it;

- Enhance transparency related to military activities and encourage publishing Defense White Papers;

- Make full use of the ASEAN Regional Forum (ARF) as a

mechanism to seek ways to eliminate instability and promote peace and stability;

- Pursue additional initiatives to defuse potential trouble areas;

- Properly handle the Taiwan question;

- Promote regional economic cooperation; and

- Enhance arms control and security research.

The remainder of this chapter provides a more detailed description of the above recommendations.

Establish Norms of State-to-State Relations

Political and diplomatic relations between states should be established and developed on the basis of the principles of mutual respect for sovereignty and territorial integrity, mutual nonaggression, noninterference in the internal affairs of other states, equality and mutual benefit, and peaceful coexistence. These five principles of peaceful coexistence, promoted by China, India, and Myanmar (the former Burma) in June 1954, have received warm support from many states and international organizations.

Their spirit was embodied in the 10 principles adopted by the Bandung Conference in 1955. They were reaffirmed by the declaration of principles of international law concerning friendly relations among states adopted by the United Nations (UN) General Assembly in 1970 and the declaration on a new international economic order adopted by the UN General Assembly in 1974. They also conform to the principles of sovereignty and equality specified in the UN Charter.

The five principles of peaceful coexistence provide a solid basis for building a new international order. They support the view that disputes between states should only be resolved peacefully through negotiation and consultation; that economic relations between states should be established and developed on the basis of equality, mutual benefit, and mutual assistance, with a view to promoting common economic development; and, finally, that all states should take a restrained attitude toward their own armament and toward military expenditures, adhering to the principle that armament should only be used for defensive purposes, in order to avert an arms race of any form.

Take an Incremental Approach

Given that most of the existing contradictions and disputes in the region are bilateral, multilateral, or regional ones, conditions are rather intricate. Because different areas and countries have different demands, an incremental approach in our search for confidence and security building is both reasonable and practicable. Bilateral arrangements should be given priority, followed by security arrangements, and then disarmament agreements. Stress should first be laid on scholarly discussions and low-level official contacts, and then on high-level meetings. Meanwhile, it is feasible to solve economic, political, and security problems through consultation and cooperation in existing regional organizations such as the Post-Ministerial Conference meeting of foreign ministers of the Association of Southeast Asian Nations (ASEAN), the Asia Pacific Economic Cooperation (APEC) Ministerial Conference, and the ASEAN Regional Forum, thus creating conditions for setting up a mechanism of consultation on security in the region in the end.

Actually, this incremental approach has already yielded many positive results in this region. Take, for example, the confrontation with massive forces along the border between China and the former Soviet Union. With the normalization of their relations, China and the former Soviet Union started talks on the reduction of border troops and on confidence building measures in 1989. In April 1990, both sides signed an agreement in principle on the mutual reduction of military forces in the border area and the strengthening of mutual trust in the military field. The "Agreement on the Eastern Section of the Sino-Soviet Border" was subsequently signed in May 1991.

After the breakup of the former Soviet Union, a joint delegation made up of Russia, Kazakhstan, Kyrgyzstan, and Tajikistan—the four members of the Commonwealth of Independent States bordering on China—continued to hold talks with China on the reduction of troops along the border. During the visit of China's president Jiang Zemin to Russia in September 1994, China and Russia issued a joint statement expressing determination to "bring bilateral relations to a new state," describing the two countries as having established "a constructive partnership of a new type," based on the five principles of peaceful coexistence and the principle of nonalignment, and not directed against any third country.

On economic, trade, scientific, and technological matters, the statement said that the two sides will make the fullest possible use of their geographical advantages and economic complementarity. It also said the two sides will explore new fields for developing economic and trade cooperation and draw up and implement a long-term plan for scientific and technological cooperation. On military and political affairs, the two sides pledged to reduce their military forces along the border to the lowest possible level and to maintain them only for defensive purposes.

The statement also said the new international order would observe the following points:

> the recognition of the diversity of the world and differences among nations; co-operation on an equal basis and participation by all countries in international affairs without discrimination; the rejection of expansionism, and the opposition to hegemonism, power politics and the establishment of antagonistic political, military and economic groups; and the settlement of disputes through peaceful negotiation, consultation and dialogue in a spirit of mutual understanding and mutual accommodation and in accordance with the principles of international law, without resorting to the threat or use of force.

China and Russia also signed a joint declaration, which announced that the two countries would no longer target strategic nuclear missiles at each other and would not use force against each other. This included a mutual no-first-use of nuclear weapons pledge. They also signed a treaty on the western Sino-Russian border and a protocol on navigation in the eastern border river.[5]

A border issue left over by history has long existed between China and India. In addition to setting up a joint team to seek ways of settlement, China and India reached an agreement on measures to build confidence along the border, including regular meetings of military personnel, the establishment of communications, and the prior notification of military exercises. Negotiations between the two sides in December 1994 approached a consensus on the reduction of their border troops. In addition, relations between China and India in the economic, trade, science, and technology fields have achieved good momentum during the past several years.

China has also developed good relations with the ASEAN states. Sino-ASEAN dialogue has been proceeding favorably for the last four years. During the 27th meeting of ASEAN foreign ministers, China signed an agreement with ASEAN on the establishment of two joint committees between ASEAN and China: the Joint Committee on Economic and Trade Cooperation, and the Joint Committee on Scientific and Technological Cooperation. China supports the ASEAN Regional Forum and believes it will promote peace and stability in the region.

Moreover, advances have been made in the increase in mutual trust and the relaxation of relations both between China and Vietnam on the border issue and between Japan and Russia on the reduction of forces stationed on the four Northern islands.[6]

Denuclearization of the Korean Peninsula

The Korean peninsula problem has had many twists and turns. On December 13, 1991, the Democratic People's Republic of Korea (DPRK) and the Republic of Korea (ROK) signed the Agreement on Reconciliation, Non-aggression and Exchanges and Cooperation. On December 31, 1991, both sides signed the Joint Declaration on the Denuclearization of the Korean Peninsula. On January 7, 1992, a South Korean Defense Ministry spokesman declared that the United States and the ROK were to suspend the 1992 Team Spirit military exercise. On the same day, the DPRK Foreign Ministry said in a statement that the government had decided to sign a nuclear safeguards agreement with the International Atomic Energy Agency (IAEA) and that it would accept IAEA inspections of its nuclear facilities. (The North actually signed on January 30). On February 19, 1992, the three inter-Korean agreements on reconciliation, denuclearization, and the establishment of a subcommittee for high-level meetings came into force upon exchange of the texts of the agreements signed by the two prime ministers.

With the inspection controversy over the DPRK nuclear program, there was a setback on the Korean peninsula. After former U.S. president Jimmy Carter visited North Korea in May 1994, the situation has gradually improved. The "Agreed Framework" reached in Geneva maintained the freeze pledged by the

DPRK in July; compliance will be monitored by IAEA inspectors. The DPRK agreed to maintain its commitment to the NPT. It also pledged to work to denuclearize the Korean peninsula. Now the United States and the DPRK are negotiating to set up liaison offices in each other's capitals and to replace a five megawatt experimental reactor with new technology considered less dangerous.

This shows that negotiation is the best way to resolve the issue of nuclear inspection in the DPRK. Sanctions are not a sensible choice, because they would only aggravate the crisis and cause the Korean people to live in misery. During the sanctions debate, China was attempting to increase its influence over North Korea by assuming a more sympathetic attitude, in order to reach a negotiated settlement. The nuclear issue mainly concerns the DPRK, the ROK, the United States, and the IAEA. If all parties continue to engage in dialogue in an equal, practical, and calm manner, and China, Russia, and Japan work together actively, the nuclear rift will be brought to a final solution.[7]

North and South Korea should be encouraged to abide by the Agreement on Reconciliation, Non-aggression and Exchanges and Cooperation and the Joint Declaration of the Denuclearization of the Korean Peninsula, which require the two sides to "eliminate political and military confrontation," to respect the principles of "non-interference in each other's internal affairs," to agree to the "non-use of force against each other," and to "settle all differences and disputes through dialogue and consultation." If both sides abide by the principles and CSBMs inherent in the above-mentioned documents, security will be ensured.

Another key to further progress lies in the normalization of U.S.-DPRK relations. In addition to the nuclear issue, the key issues are transformation of the Armistice Agreement into a peace treaty and the phased withdrawal of U.S. forces and military bases from South Korea. It deserves commendation that the United States has withdrawn all land-based tactical nuclear weapons deployed in South Korea and that the United States and the DPRK are prepared to establish diplomatic representation in each other's capitals and reduce barriers to trade and investment as moves toward full normalization of political and economic relations. It is self-evident that the Big Four—the United States, Russia, China, and Japan—should do everything possible to help facilitate the denuclearization of the Korean peninsula and the safeguarding of peace and stability in the area.

No-First-Use/Nuclear-Weapon-Free Zones

All nuclear states should reach an agreement undertaking not to be the first to use nuclear weapons in any circumstances and not to use or threaten to use nuclear weapons against non-nuclear-weapon states or in nuclear-weapon-free zones. If we are all keen on establishing CSBMs, why not establish CSBMs in such an important field as preventing a nuclear war? Based on experience from the Chemical Weapons Convention, a no-first-use agreement would be an important step towards the total ban of nuclear weapons. The 1925 Geneva Protocol on chemical weapons is, in fact, a no-first-use agreement that evolved into a total ban. If an agreement on no-first-use of nuclear weapons could be reached, it would be an important breakthrough in nuclear arms control. Under these circumstances, the United States and Russia could abandon their extended nuclear deterrence and reduce their nuclear arsenals further, and the medium nuclear states would join in the nuclear disarmament process. This would reduce the role of nuclear weapons in world politics and promote the establishment of nuclear-weapon-free zones in the region.

In Northeast Asia, the Korean peninsula should be denuclearized and a nuclear-weapon-free zone should be established. In Southeast Asia, support should be given to the ASEAN proposition concerning the creation of a Zone of Peace, Freedom, and Neutrality (ZOPFAN) in Southeast Asia and the establishment of a Southeast Asian nuclear-weapon-free zone in order to enhance peace, security, and stability in this area. In South Asia, the South Asian nuclear-weapon-free zone and the Indian Ocean peace zone should be established, so as to achieve denuclearization in this region.

In recent years, progress has been made in the area of confidence building measures in South Asia. India and Pakistan have reached an official agreement on mutual non-attack on nuclear facilities, the establishment of direct contacts between higher military departments, and the setting up of a system of prior notification of military exercises. But Pakistani opposition leader Nawaz Sharif has claimed that Pakistan possesses an atom bomb. Although quickly denied by the government of Benazir Bhutto, this statement has worsened Pakistan's strained relationship with India. The Pakistani government's stand has always been that it has the ability to produce nuclear weapons, but that it has made a policy decision not to make one. India, which exploded a nuclear device in 1974, says it does not have a bomb. Prime Minister Narasimha Rao has said India would keep its nuclear option open. Both states remain out of the NPT and this will become an obstacle to that universal regime on nonproliferation.

If all nuclear states could reach an agreement undertaking not to be the first to use nuclear weapons in any circumstances and not to use or threaten to use nuclear weapons against non-nuclear-weapon states or nuclear-weapon-free zones, it would encourage India and Pakistan to participate in the NPT and help create favorable conditions for the establishment of the nuclear-weapon-free zone in South Asia.

Extend the Missile Technology Control Regime

At present, the MTCR is neither an international treaty nor a normal agreement; it is merely an understanding that identical lists of items will be placed on the export control lists of the member states. If a non-member state violates the MTCR, the United States would also apply sanctions against it. In theory, all states have the sovereign right to develop and deploy whatever weapon systems they judge will enhance their security. Thus it can be argued that it is illegitimate to place constraints on these capabilities other than those voluntarily accepted.

In the developing world there is general agreement that the developed world often neglects the legitimate security interests of other states. Coupled to this is the view that the developed world employs double standards when it comes to policies concerning nuclear, chemical, and biological weapons and their delivery vehicles; their position is seen as one of "do as we say, not as we do." Indeed, the MTCR is essentially a suppliers' diktat imposed by a few developed states on the developing ones to contain the transfer of technology that might contribute to ballistic missile systems.[8]

The MTCR is obviously unfair and unreasonable for two reasons. First, because ballistic missiles are delivery vehicles and not weapons of mass destruction per se, there is an issue over why they should be treated any differently from advanced military strike aircraft, which can also deliver weapons of mass destruction, and over which there have been no comparable proposals for control. Many Western countries have sold and are still selling such aircraft. Second, the MTCR is controlled by a few Western states. The United States can sell Trident strategic missiles to Britain, but other member or non-member states that sell ballistic missiles over the limits set by the MTCR will be subjected to sanctions.

I support nonproliferation of ballistic missiles, but the control system should be built on a fair, reasonable, comprehensive basis. As a Chinese proverb says, "Whatever you are not willing to do, do not force the other to do." My suggestion is to extend the MTCR to a treaty encompassing limitations on all aspects of nuclear, chemical, and biological weapons delivery vehicles of all types. All participants should enjoy equal rights to discuss and settle problems related to the control regime. We can learn from the NPT, which seeks to fulfil three objectives: to contain the number of states possessing nuclear weapons; to provide an international framework for nuclear trading; and to contribute to the general process of arms limitation and disarmament. The effective operation of the NPT requires a balance between all three objectives. Obviously, the nonproliferation of delivery vehicles also requires the same balance.

Under a Federation of American Scientists' plan for ballistic missile disarmament, the United States and Russia would agree on a contingent "good faith initiative" to make substantial further reductions in missiles if all nations would agree, at a world conference, to attempt the goal of zero ballistic missiles. Thereafter eight regional zones covering the entire world would attempt freezes and disarmament of ballistic missiles in their regions.[9] I believe this proposal would be well received by the developing world.

Enhance Transparency .

Transparency is not an end in itself, but a means to an end. Transparency can help to reduce fear of aggressive arms acquisitions or intent, and thus help promote regional or global peace, security, and stability. But, as Brad Roberts and Robert Ross observe in this volume's closing chapter, "transparency is not a universal good." The effect of transparency is different for militarily strong countries than it is for militarily weak countries. For the former, transparency can serve to enhance their deterrence; for the latter, transparency may expose their vulnerabilities. Thus we should encourage countries in the region to publish Defense White Papers, consistent with their specific conditions.

In view of the allegation that the "threat from China has spread like wildfire" and has thus been harmful to regional stability, it is essential for China to publish a Defense White Paper. Threat allegations refer specifically to China's increase in military expenditures and to planned purchases of aircraft carriers, advanced fighters, and so on. But, take the increase in military expenditure as an example. China's military expenditures have long been maintained at a lower level. In recent years, they have increased annually by over 10 percent, but this increase has been mainly due to inflation and the appropriate improvement of the living standard of military personnel.

China's total military expenditures for 1992 amounted to only $6.85 billion, making up 1.6 percent of the gross national product (GNP), and for 1993 amounted to only $7.3 billion, making up 1.5 percent of the GNP. Such a figure cannot compare with the military expenditures of tens or hundreds of billions of U.S. dollars by some big powers in the world. It is even lower than some of China's neighbors, such as Japan, the ROK, and India.

In addition, in the early 1980s China started on a large scale to convert its defense industries from manufacturing military items to making products for civilian use. At present, 70 percent of the output value of China's defense industries are products for civilian use. The profits from these products do not go to the army but are, instead, used for national economic development. China is now concentrating on its economic development and needs a peaceful international environment. Facts have illustrated that China's so-called "arms expansion" and "the threat from China" are utterly groundless. I believe a Chinese Defense White Paper would clarify some facts and clear up misunderstandings.

Make Full Use of the ASEAN Regional Forum

Seeing that conditions are not ripe for setting up a mechanism for consultation on security for the whole region, we can utilize the ARF to discuss regional security related to every country and CSBMs in the region. Preliminary bilateral or multilateral CSBMs could include the following:

- No-first-use of force declarations;

- Publication and exchange of defense budgets and force structure details;

- Prior notification of military maneuver and troop movements along the border;

- Exchanges of high-level defense officials;

- Hot lines and cool lines for immediate consultation in crises.

Pursue Additional Initiatives

In addition, the following CSBMs are proposed to defuse potential trouble areas and alleviate regional concerns.

Settle the South China Sea issue peacefully.   According to China's claim, the sea areas of China's South Sea and its islands have fallen within China's domain since as far back as A.D. 789. China's position is to settle disputes through peaceful talks. If conditions are not yet ripe for talks, then the disputes should be shelved and nations should cooperate to jointly exploit the natural resources of the disputed territories.[10] This view echoes the 1992 ASEAN declaration. Where conflicts have deep historical roots, non-military measures such as the joint exploitation of resources and cooperative development programs might be more appropriate. Under present circumstances, shelving the disputes is the best way. The next generation will be wiser and will better understand how to solve them fairly.

Encourage all coastal states in the region to sign and ratify the UN Convention on the Law of the Sea.   The Convention consolidates delimitation rules governing disputes of coastal states concerning territorial waters, contiguous areas, exclusive economic zones, continental shelf areas, islands, and international shipping channels. The convention will be binding on ratifying and participating states and will provide a mechanism for the settlement of disputes.

Seek the conclusion of a multilateral accord based on the U.S.-Soviet Incidents at Sea Agreement.   The U.S.-Soviet agreement gives prominence to a strict limit on threats and provocation. For example, it stipulates that "ships of the parties shall not simulate attack, by aiming guns, missile launchers, torpedo tubes, and other weapons in the direction of a passing ship of the other party, not launch any object in the direction of passing ships of the other party, and not use searchlights or other power- ful illumination devices to illuminate the navigation bridges of passing ships of the other party." This is warmly regarded by coastal states that have long looked forward to a treaty of this kind to ensure them of protection from provocations. Moreover, the agreement is confined only to the prevention of incidents on and over the high seas. It is related neither to arms control, which directly concerns a nation's security and stability, nor to disarmament-related confidence building measures, such as exchanges of information and on-site observation. A multilateral accord based on the U.S.-Soviet agreement would not impinge upon the security concerns of any regional states, thus it is easily acceptable to the states concerned.[11] Initially, such an accord could be negotiated on a bilateral basis. Eventually, a series of bilateral accords could provide the basis for a multilateral accord.

Pay close attention to Japan's nuclear program. Japan is an economic superpower and is moving toward becoming a world political power. Although Japanese political leaders have time and again declared that Japan will not be a big military power posing a threat to neighboring countries, Asian countries that suffered untold hardships from Japanese aggression in the past are very concerned over Japan's future military policy and orien- tation. In this connection, there is a trend in Japan worthy of attention: namely, the continuous accumulation of plutonium of power reactor grade. In 20 years, Japan will have accumulated the greatest quantity of plutonium of power reactor grade in the world, estimated to be up to 80 to 90 tons. By then Japan will have consumed no more than 20 to 40 tons of plutonium in its power reactor, with 40 to 50 tons of industrial plutonium remain- ing. This kind of plutonium can be used to make crude atomic bombs. Moreover, Japan is developing a laser isotope separation method, which could convert industrial plutonium into weapon grade plutonium to make advanced nuclear weapons. One cannot help but be concerned about why the Japanese are accumulating so much plutonium. It seems necessary now to set up an international storage system for the separated plutonium. The best option would be for Japan (and other countries) to abandon their plutonium plans, because they are economically unsustainable and raise serious security and proliferation concerns.

Handle the Taiwan Question Properly

The Taiwan question is an internal affair of China, which should not even be discussed in this chapter. There is, however, a trend toward the internationalization of the Taiwan question that would disturb the careful equilibrium provided by the current "one country, two systems" formula; this would lead to instability in the region.

Taiwan, a province of China, is an inalienable part of Chinese territory. UN General Assembly resolution 2758, adopted at its 26th session in 1971, stated that it recognizes "that the representatives of the Government of the People's Republic of China are the only lawful representatives of China to the United Nations." Taiwan authorities, however, have recently conducted so-called elastic diplomacy, in essence designed to create "two Chinas" or "one China, one Taiwan."

China does not object to the nongovernmental economic and cultural exchanges between Taiwan and other countries, but China is firmly opposed to actions that undermine China's sovereignty and territorial integrity and jeopardize peaceful reunification.

The principle of peaceful reunification has already been set. The mainland's refusal to abandon the possible use of force is aimed only at foreign aggressors and Taiwanese independence activists. It is unrealistic to demand that Taiwan change its existing system, either. According to the "one China, two systems" concept, the mainland will not send a soldier to Taiwan after reunification; the existing party, government, and army systems will remain unchanged. Certainly, it will take a long time to reach this goal. Given economic development and reform on the mainland and ongoing economic and cultural exchange between the people on both sides of the Taiwan Strait, however, reunification will be realized sooner or later.

The Taiwan authorities' change concerning the "one China" policy also stems from international influences. As we discuss CSBMs for the Asia Pacific region, the U.S. sale of F-16s and other sophisticated weapons to Taiwan and the upgrading of U.S. relations with Taiwan, along with Japan's allowing Taiwan's "Vice-President of the Executive Yuan" Hsu Li-teh to enter Japan are no CSBMs. They will do no good to either side of the Taiwan

Strait or to the United States or Japan. No state in the region wants the two sides of the Taiwan Strait to experience a time of chaos, which may lead to overall regional instability. The Chinese people wish the United States, Japan, and all friendly states would do everything possible to help facilitate the peaceful reunification of China.

Promote Regional Economic Cooperation

Economic, scientific, and technological cooperation and trade would assist in the development of interdependence, mutual trust, and confidence. This, in turn, would create a sense of community among the regional states in which the role of force would be minimized. Indeed, this is already the case in the Asia Pacific. Most countries and regions in the area have long since given priority to domestic economic development. This has helped bring about a virtuous circle of mutual promotion between political stability and economic development. Last year, 34 conflicts occurred worldwide, but only six were in the Asia Pacific region. So far this year, 35 clashes have occurred worldwide, with just five located in the Asia Pacific region.[12] Facts prove that the economic element is very important for world stability and security. There are good prospects for the Asia Pacific regional economy.

China's imports should grow considerably from now until the turn of the century; total imports will amount to more than $1,000 billion. China is the largest consumer market for the factories of the world. Along with China's reentry into the General Agreement on Tariffs and Trade, the world market would become more brisk. With the vast market and relatively stable political situation, it is possible for the region to maintain rapid development. Many people believe that the Asia Pacific region will become the most important part of the world by the end of the century.

Enhance Arms Control and Security Research

In contrast with the Western countries, arms control and security research in the developing world lags behind in Asia. For instance, there is no professional institute for arms control research in China; only a few people do research in this field and most of them do it part-time. Obviously, it is necessary to establish professional institutes and to develop professional skills. In addition, educational exchange among countries should be enhanced. All of these will be beneficial to confidence and security building in the region.

Notes

1.   Chen Wenqing, "Security Situation in the Asia-Pacific Region and the Possibility of Confidence-and Security-building Measures," *International Strategic Studies*, no. 2 (1991).

2.   See Yasushi Akashi (UN under secretary general for Disarmament Affairs), "Step-by-Step Confidence-building for Asian-Pacific Region," *Disarmament Topical Papers 6*, United Nations Publication, 1991.

3.   Cathleen S. Fisher, "The Preconditions of Confidence-building: Lessons from the European Experience," in Michael Krapon, ed., *A Handbook of Confidence-building Measures for Regional Security* (Washington, D.C.: Henry L. Stimson Center, 1993).

4.   Alexei V. Zagorsky, "North-East Asian Security- and Confidence-building," *Disarmament Topical Papers 6*, 1991. Zagorsky is from the Centre for Japanese and Pacific Studies, Institute of World Economy and International Relations in Moscow.

5.   See "Joint Statement Fosters Sino-Russian Relations," and "Jiang: Enhanced Ties Will Ensure Peace, Stability," *China Daily*, September 5, 1994.

6.   Luo Renshi, "New Situation of Arms Control and Disarmament in the Asia-Pacific Region and China's Policy and Course of Action," *International Strategic Studies*, no. 1 (1993).

7.   Personally, I am optimistic about the future in the Korean peninsula. It seems that North Korea will gradually open up to the outside world, undergo reform, and concentrate on its economic development. The problem will be solved, and we need not be overanxious.

8.   Darryl Howlett and John Simpson, "Dangers in the 1990's: Nuclear, Chemical and Biological Weapons and Missile Proliferation," *Disarmament Topical Papers 6*, 1991.

9.   *Federation of American Scientists Public Interest Report*, Washington, D.C., March/April 1994.

10.   "China: No Need for Special Security Body," *China Daily*, July 24, 1994.

11.   Jin Shouqi, "An Analysis of the Current Bilateral and Multilateral Maritime Confidence-building Measures," *Disarmament Topical Papers 4*, 1990.

12.   Wang Yonghong, "Asia Boom Promotes Stability," *China Daily*, May 27, 1994.

8

Confidence and Security Building Measures: A USCSCAP Task Force Report

Brad Roberts and Robert Ross

In spring 1994, the United States Committee of the Council on Security Cooperation in the Asia Pacific (USCSCAP) formed a task force on confidence and security building measures (CSBMs) with three purposes in mind. First, it seeks to support the dialogue on CSBMs recently initiated within the context of the ASEAN (Association of Southeast Asian Nations) Regional Forum (ARF).[1] Second, it seeks to facilitate the implementation of CSBMs elsewhere in the Asia Pacific, whether in subregions such as Northeast Asia or across the entire region. Third, it seeks to stimulate and inform thinking about long-term trends in the region and their implications for regional security among the interested public.

Defining CSBMs

When the debate about CSBMs began in the Asia Pacific approximately a decade ago, a rather narrow and specific meaning was attributed to them. They were generally defined as those measures adopted in Europe and formalized under the aegis of the Conference on Security and Cooperation in Europe (CSCE) for increasing transparency among adversaries and diminishing suspicions of aggressive intent. Pundits proposed simply lifting these measures from their European context and grafting them onto the Asia Pacific nations.

Security specialists in the Asia Pacific rightly rejected such notions as far too narrow an understanding of CSBMs. But the debate begun by such proposals has proven helpful in focusing thinking within the region about its long-term security. Particularly in Southeast Asia, that debate has now progressed to a point where measures can be crafted and implemented that offer promise of making a meaningful contribution to regional security.

We wish to underscore as a point of departure that CSBMs are not a panacea. They do not solve basic conflicts of interest.

Nor is transparency a universal good.[2] But even when CSBMs fail, lessons can be drawn from their failure and the stakes of conflict are clarified. The utility of CSBMs is not the elimination of conflict. Rather, it is to help states to narrow and defuse potential conflicts among them and to help ensure that when and if war does occur, it is a result of genuine conflicts of interest and not of mistakes or accidents.

We also observe that CSBMs are not the only things that generate confidence and security among nations. Alliances and security guarantees play an important role, especially in Northeast Asia, in providing both confidence and security; but they are not properly defined as CSBMs. Regional economic cooperation and integration into the global trading system also generate confidence and shared interests but they do not constitute CSBMs either. Within the Asia Pacific, we note with particular concern the uncertainty about the future roles of the great powers and relations among them. Without complementary diplomatic and security strategies aimed at sustaining the fundamental aspects of a concert or balance among these powers, CSBMs will be able to contribute little or nothing to regional security.

As a task force of the United States Committee, we recognize in particular that the United States is both part of the problem and part of the solution in the Asia Pacific, given the questions asked throughout the region about the nature of its long-term commitment and engagement. Uncertainty about the U.S. global role and its historical tendency toward isolationism, its growing economic combativeness, and the occasional hint of imperiousness all work against the achievement of shared aspirations for a secure and cooperative regional order. Indeed, we see our task as an ingredient of a larger effort to expound a U.S. vision of a better Asia Pacific community in which everyone benefits.

This task force adopts an expansive definition of CSBMs as including both formal and informal measures, whether unilateral, bilateral, or multilateral, that address, prevent, and resolve uncertainties among states. It conceives of CSBMs as including both military and political elements relevant for the larger and longer-term task of creating a Security Community. Generically speaking, CSBMs have a number of functions.[3] They create habits of cooperation and patterns of communication that contribute to greater clarity about the orientations, ambitions, and capabilities of neighboring states. This may contribute to a reduction of uncertainty, misperception, and suspicion; it may also bring into focus abiding conflicts or deep differences of strategic orientation that keep suspicion alive, but we deem this a useful result and one that may contribute to peace when such conflicts can be managed or aggression deterred. Some CSBMs have also been crafted that strengthen the capacity of participating nations to manage high-stakes crises that threaten to erupt into war. Some CSBMs also help to reduce the possibility of incidental or accidental war. Transparency mechanisms may reduce fear of aggressive arms acquisitions or intent. Dialogue mechanisms may buy time to defuse crises, avoid escalation, and create a favorable environment for permanent peace agreements.

Our concept of CSBMs also includes the formal treaty regimes that have been negotiated and implemented globally, such as the Nuclear Non-Proliferation Treaty (NPT), the Biological and Toxin Weapons Convention (BWC), and the United Nations (UN) Register of Conventional Arms. The fundamental purpose of these regimes is to create stable relations among nations by building confidence about their commitment to agreed norms of behavior, to weapons programs oriented toward defensive and not offensive purposes, and to collective responses to threats to these norms. Where doubts about treaty compliance exist, as in North Korea and elsewhere in the world, the confidence generated by these treaties is eroded, and rumblings echo through the region of a future diffusion of weapons of mass destruction.

CSBMs are important for what they make possible among nations. CSBMs in Europe contributed to the transformation of relations between West and East, in the Middle East to recent breakthroughs in the Arab-Israeli peace process, and in Latin America to burgeoning economic relations. But we would also argue that it is not important to have the end very firmly in sight when beginning to work with a CSBM strategy. Indeed, the experience with CSBMs elsewhere in the world suggests that states generally do not have a clear, long-term goal in mind when adopting CSBMs, other than to take constructive steps to shape conflicts in ways that keep them manageable. CSBMs were adopted during the height of the cold war to keep the U.S.-Soviet nuclear competition from pitching both into nuclear Armageddon, with little sense of what would follow in the 1970s and 1980s in the way of formal arms control mechanisms. CSBMs have been in place in the Middle East since the 1960s and have helped make possible a much more ambitious agenda in a post-cold war environment. In Latin America, bilateral CSBMs between Argentina and Brazil have led over a decade to an entirely new and rigorous nuclear arms control mechanism—and played an important role in securing the transitions to civilian rule. This experience suggests that states facing a rapidly changing and highly volatile international security environment have opted to implement limited CSBMs without knowing where they would end up years or decades later. The most successful efforts at establishing CSBMs have begun with the least controversial and ambitious initiatives.

CSBMs are important not just because they are means to an end; the means themselves are valuable. Dialogue for dialogue's sake has had a subtle effect everywhere CSBMs have been tried in redefining perceptions, bringing shared interests into focus, and creating new connections among peoples.

Some in the Asia Pacific reject CSBMs as a Western contrivance. The facts do not support this interpretation. In both Latin America and the Middle East, and to a lesser extent in South Asia, leaders have created CSBMs with a mix of borrowed and indigenous elements. Indeed, in each of these regions, there has been a good deal more activism than in the Asia Pacific in utilizing and adapting such measures—this despite early widespread opposition to CSBMs as unsuited to regional needs (an argument often heard in the Asia Pacific). Even in the West, concepts and methods employed under the CSBM rubric have evolved over time; we note particularly the post-cold war "cooperative threat reduction" program of the United States and Russia as a new form of cooperation that transcends existing definitions of CSBMs and arms control.

A final comment on terminology: we note the search within the region for indigenously derived substitutes for the term "CSBM." We have no quarrel with terms such as "mutual reassurance measures" and "trust building measures" if they make the CSBM agenda more palatable to officials and analysts within the region. But, because terms do have an importance of their own, whatever term comes into vogue should keep people focused on security as the long-term priority that makes the interim measures important.

Understanding the Place of CSBMs in the Asia Pacific

Why are CSBMs important for the Asia Pacific? We believe that there are three strong arguments in support of an activist CSBM agenda.

First, the nations of the region must chart a new course for the future if they are to continue to reap the benefits of the economic fraternity that has developed among them. This is well recognized today in Southeast Asia, where the ASEAN dialogue on regional security represents a turning point for nations that heretofore have considered security to be a topic reserved for solely national discussion. In Northeast Asia, this is also true but less recognized, given the great uncertainties associated with future relations among states in the region and their long-term nuclear weapons potential. Throughout the larger region, business as usual may not be enough to prevent economic frictions from coalescing with domestic instabilities and disputed borders in ways that harm shared long-term economic and political interests.

Looked at in large historical terms, the region is being swept by forces unleashed by its own rapid development and by the end of the cold war. There is profound uncertainty about the role of the major powers, such as China, Japan, Russia, and the United States, among others, and a sense that a decade or two hence a very different constellation of relations might prevail among these powers. There are numerous unresolved territorial disputes that could flare into hot war if left too long untended or otherwise mishandled. The use of force in support of diplomacy remains legitimate in the region, not nearly to the same degree as in the Middle East, but far more so than in Latin America. Many states are struggling with their own weaknesses to meet the challenges of rapidly changing societies; many societies are coping with the stresses unleashed by rapid modernization.

Despite a growing sense of regional (or subregional) identity, there is no habit of formal multilateralism among states in the Asia Pacific that elsewhere, as in Latin America and Europe, has facilitated the creation of new international mechanisms to cope with new shared problems. Moreover, the proliferation of high-leverage weapons to some states in the region, a broader diffusion of the defense industrial base (and of the technologies necessary for weapons of mass destruction), and the regionwide growth of defense budgets over the past decade hold out the potential for a far less stable and much higher-risk security environment in years or decades hence.[4]

Let us underscore, however, that our view of the region today is extremely positive. Seen in global context, the Asia Pacific stands out as a region where positive trends and possibilities far outweigh negative trends and lingering problems. Rapid and sustained economic growth have deepened contacts among states in the region, creating many shared interests and a habit of cooperation and consultation. The security environment is generally benign. The problem of war in the region is by and large a problem of civil war in a few spots; rare are the sources of international conflict that might erupt into armed combat.

But we also view the Asia Pacific as a microcosm of the fundamental post-cold war issue: Will the emergent world order be one dominated by the shared interests and patterns of cooperation arising from patterns of complex interdependence among states and societies, so that security conflicts are addressed and resolved through consultations and negotiations? In short, is a genuine Security Community possible, firmly rooted in a balance of power among nations and in effective implementation of both comprehensive and cooperative security agendas? Or will the release of long-suppressed tensions combine with the struggle for a new balance of power in the region to poison patterns of cooperation, erode shared interests, and precipitate over time the emergence of competitive hegemonies that resort to war where their interests collide? The concern that the latter pattern may prevail in the Asia Pacific is well established.[5]

This task force makes no prediction about which trend will prevail in the long term. But the existing level and quality of dialogue and regional institutionalization appear insufficient to meet these looming challenges or to keep the community of nations in the region focused on their shared interests. The utility of CSBMs is precisely in preventing long-term problems from taking shape in ways that overwhelm the capacity to deal with them. The development of CSBMs can be part of the process of building multilateralism. For these reasons we reject the argument that advocates of CSBMs in the Asia Pacific are pushing a solution for which there is no problem. Instead, we call for an activist CSBM agenda for the very reason that it will help to shape trends in the region in ways conducive to preservation of the existing relatively benign environment.

Second, there are a host of specific problems in the region for which CSBMs would be constructive adjuncts to existing diplomatic, security, economic, and political mechanisms. CSBMs could be useful in dealing with some of the questions about the great powers, by facilitating long-term U.S. engagement in the region and greater Chinese openness and commitment to multilateralism, and by easing the frictions associated with the simultaneous emergence of China and Japan as great powers. CSBMs could be useful in preventing border disputes from turning into wars and more generally for mitigating the effects of historical animosities. They could also be useful in preventing military modernization programs from generating arms races, the growth of mutual mistrust, and a movement toward unconventional weapons capabilities. They could also help to manage common problems created by piracy, drug trafficking, and terrorism.

Some doubt whether perceptions of the regional security agenda converge sufficiently to permit the functioning of CSBMs. Indeed, we cannot but be struck by the great variety of threat perceptions among states in the region. But as this list of specific problems demonstrates, interests do converge on an issue-by-issue basis. Moreover, there are also a number of important shared interests that can provide the basis for sustained multilateral cooperation in continued economic growth; in domestic political stability and legitimacy; in the management of international relations in ways that prevent serious disruptions of national development strategies; and in preventing relations among the major powers from degenerating into all-out armaments racing and competition for influence. The contrast between divergent perceptions and shared interests only underscores the importance of using the current period of reduced tension to build the foundation for future cooperation.

Third, the region already has a valuable, if often overlooked, record of implementing CSBMs that should serve as a solid foundation for a more ambitious agenda. These include a variety of informal mechanisms such as military-to-military dialogues; formal bilateral measures such as border commissions or the Japanese-Russian Incidents at Sea agreement; multilateral measures such as the South Pacific Nuclear Free Zone (SPNFZ) or the regional parliamentary forum; and unilateral measures, such as declarations of principles or troop redeployments away from conflict zones. In addition, the contribution of ASEAN as a successful CSBM should not be overlooked. By providing a mechanism for the original member-countries to stabilize their often fractious international relationships, ASEAN allowed them to turn their attention to combating serious domestic challenges and then to focusing on economic development.[6]

This history provides a valuable lesson for the future: CSBMs must be suited to the strategic realities and cultures that prevail in the region. Strategic realities of special relevance for CSBMs include the following: the development of multipolarity among the regional powers; gross disparities of power across the region; a reluctance among the strong to empower the weak through multilateral mechanisms; the weak roots of multilateralism in the region; and the absence of any widely shared sense of a true Asia Pacific community. These realities mean that a formal mechanism such as the CSCE cannot productively be implemented in the region at this time. Fragmented leadership, lack of consensus regarding the sources of instability, and recent history combine to make collective action exceedingly difficult. Among the elements of strategic culture germane to the CSBM topic are the following: an emphasis on pragmatism and consensus building; a preference for informal structures of policy-making; a stronger emphasis on personal relationships than on formal legal structures; a deep commitment to the principle of noninterference; a predilection to think in the context of distant time horizons and of gradual and incremental approaches to problems; and a generational change now beginning in the leadership ranks. If adequately taken into account, these factors lend themselves extremely well to the development in the Asia Pacific of multilateral security cooperation.

The ARF has already specified an agenda "for further study." To cite the Chairman's Statement concerning the July 1994 meeting:

> The meeting also agreed to entrust the next Chairman of the ARF, Brunei Darussalem, working in consultation with ARF participants as appropriate, to a) collate and study all papers and ideas raised during the ARF Senior Officials Meeting. . . . Ideas which might be the subjects of study include confidence and security building, nuclear non-proliferation, peacekeeping cooperation including regional peacekeeping training centres, exchanges of non-classified military information, maritime security issues, and preventive diplomacy; b) study the comprehensive concept of security, including its economic and social aspects, as it pertains to the Asia Pacific region; c) study other relevant internationally recognized norms and principles pertaining to international and regional political and security cooperation for their possible contribution to regional political and security cooperation; d) promote the eventual participation of all ARF countries in the UN Conventional Arms Register; and e) convene, if necessary, informal meetings of the officials.[7]

This ambitious beginning should provide the impetus for a gradual implementation of a more ambitious CSBM agenda within the region in the context of larger diplomatic and political strategies to promote regional security. The mandate of this task force is to help define the CSBM component of a more comprehensive approach to the management of regional security that ultimately will have many components: preserving the balance of power; managing crises; building trust; managing common security concerns; resolving disputes; and identifying and responding to emerging political, economic, environmental, and demographic threats. CSBMs offer the opportunity to build on existing foundations to achieve grander goals in the decades ahead.

Recommendations

Analysts and officials have produced many lists of possible CSBMs for the region. This task force believes that it would be useful to concentrate debate and diplomatic energy on the following specific measures. We have sought to identify both short-term and long-term priorities, in order to highlight those initiatives with immediate benefits for the region and to focus thinking about future possibilities if success is won in early efforts. We also discuss a number of measures often featured in the regional CSBM debate that would be counterproductive for regional confidence and security if too aggressively pursued at this time.

1. Expand Transparency Measures Related to Politico-Military Matters

Suspicions about the capabilities and intent of neighboring states, especially those with which a disputed border is shared, are often fueled by the prevailing climate of secrecy. Where that secrecy does not harbor aggressive intent, states would be well served by making the thinking and actions of the military community more visible to others. As noted earlier, the degree of transparency that provides security without compromising other interests (such as, potentially, a degree of uncertainty about forces held in reserve, etc., in the name of deterrence) varies from case to case. But the region appears ripe for a significant commitment to transparency. The only caveat is that, as in other areas, the initial groundwork remains to be laid. Thus, first steps to multilateral commitments to transparency will require initial unilateral and bilateral efforts on the part of influential regional states. As suggested below, many of these steps are tied to the Defense White Paper process.

Specific measures include the following:

(a) Existing military-to-military contacts should be expanded. Surveying the entire region we find many examples of a pattern of expanding dialogue and cooperation across national boundaries, along with considerable momentum in this process. But the pattern is incomplete and the momentum subject to disruption. More such contacts, in both formal and informal settings, would help to build up relationships, develop habits of consultation, and identify areas of cooperation on shared interests.

(b) States should agree to minimum standards of openness with regard to national security policy. A formal questionnaire should be developed that, once completed, would be circulated to participating nations and made available publicly. This would have the most short-term benefit in Southeast Asia but the definition of a norm and procedure could be implemented elsewhere in the region. At a minimum, the information to be provided by participating states should include data on major weapons procurement programs, a summary of national security strategy, notification of changes in military doctrine, and advance notice of weapons acquisitions that significantly increase the range or sophistication of military forces. This should complement but go beyond information provided to the UN and regional arms registers. Complementary initiatives could include some or all of the following: exchanges on what is already made public; exchanges among military planners; and greater openness in the policy-making process perhaps, for example, through more public parliamentary review.

(c) States should offer unilateral commitments to open up their military establishments while pressing others in the region to do the same. Beyond the contacts among military leaders referred to above, such commitments could include the opening of exercises over a certain numerical threshold to international inspection, and the preparation of annual calendars of military exercises, all in conjunction with the publication of Defense White Papers. Australia's commitments in this domain should be followed by others. Such commitments are helpful not just because they

diminish the risk of surprise attack but because they also make war less thinkable by humanizing the enemy. One variation on this approach would be a commitment to open for challenge inspection by a neutral international team any military facility that raises suspicions in the minds of a neighbor, perhaps in exchange for a promise of reciprocal rights.

(d) States should add questions of defense strategy and weapons procurement to the list of topics for discussion among governmental representatives in non-public venues. Discussions at the peer level of national security policy-making and military doctrine and plans could contribute usefully to greater comfort with the high levels of defense spending in the region. The task force notes that the ASEAN Regional Forum has already received a proposal to develop a working group to consider such military exchanges; it urges the Regional Forum to move rapidly to establish this working group.

(e) The region should create a regional arms register that goes beyond what is possible in the UN context. Such a register would provide more detailed information and entail stricter reporting requirements. The region has already moved in this direction on economic flows under the auspices of the Asia Pacific Economic Cooperation (APEC) forum. This proposal echoes a 1992 Malaysian proposal for a regional register that would solicit data not just on transfers but also on holdings, categories of weapons not included in the UN register (such as small arms—an increasingly important part of the arms market), and financial terms of sale (so as to determine the incentives for sales). Argentina has made a proposal of a similar nature for South America.

This is important for the following reasons. Asia is on track to become the most heavily armed region in the world.[8] Patterns of armaments acquisition in the region reveal sustained high levels of defense spending, although most such spending is defensible in terms of needs to modernize existing forces or protect maritime economic zones. But there is no guarantee that continued high rates of military spending will be as defensible. The growing sophistication, strategic reach, and sheer size of regional militaries may prove destabilizing if this creates new fears and new connections between heretofore separate theaters. The diffusion of high-leverage weapons will accelerate the diffusion of power within the region and the declining influence of the great powers. Such capabilities also cast growing doubt on the credibility of alliance guarantees and threats of collective security actions by raising their potential costs in time of war. We are also particularly concerned that the region not emerge as a major source of weapons and weapons-related technologies on world markets.

Thus some mechanism must be created for governments and nongovernmental specialists (both in the region and outside it) to discuss patterns of defense spending and weapons acquisition. Agreement that certain types of acquisitions are stabilizing or destabilizing will be as elusive in the Asia Pacific as in the Middle East, but some better understanding of armaments flows in the region would help to identify areas of concern and inform a debate about implications. It is not in the interest of states of the Asia Pacific to allow a pattern of relatively benign armaments acquisition to degrade into corrosive arms races—or an extremely complex set of such races. Simply trusting that modernization will not prove destabilizing is too risky in a region so rich in embittered histories and contested borders.

(f) The emergence of more informed and sophisticated public debate about questions of regional security should be facilitated by governments. In the United States, Europe, and South Asia, nongovernmental organizations have emerged as generators of new thinking about problems of international security. They have been a resource for governments to turn to for those ideas, or to test new thinking of their own. They have also played an important societal role in raising the level of debate in the media and academe on questions of public policy. But the culture that prevails in many parts of the Asia Pacific works against the emergence of such institutions in these roles beyond their existing narrow confines. Some greater willingness of governments to open their thinking to public discussion and to provide the data necessary for informed discussion would have positive security repercussions over the medium and long term throughout the region.

The USCSCAP task force wishes to add its voice to those opposing a formal, comprehensive, regionwide transparency mechanism analogous to the CSCE. This is neither possible nor desirable. But we believe that subregional measures, perhaps quite varied in nature, would be desirable and possible in the long term.

2. Build on Existing Habits of Practical Cooperation on a Diverse Set of Public Policy Issues with Long-Term Security-related Implications

(a) Create a maritime cooperation regime or regimes and develop existing maritime cooperation even further.   The existing experience of the region with maritime cooperation is distinctive even as future maritime challenges are increasing in number. A broad array of measures have been put in place in recent years, including not just traditional CSBMs such as bilateral military exercises but also broader cooperation on maritime safety and surveillance.[9] To a certain degree, these are classic transparency measures. But they also touch on operational aspects—and in any case deserve special prominence because of the uniquely maritime character of the Asia Pacific security environment. Some strengthening of this approach is warranted. Specifically, existing ad hoc bilateral naval exercises should be increased in number and formalized where possible.

We also recommend creation of a maritime safety and sur-veillance regime. States of the region face a common challenge in maintaining the security of the sea lines of communication and the general safety of the maritime environment. A more coordi-nated and formalized approach to the task of policing the seas would bring many political benefits. Such an approach might focus on measures to combat smuggling and piracy, to prevent or control incidents at sea that might lead to war, to monitor pol-lution, and to provide common search and rescue capabilities.[10] One possible mechanism would be multilateralization of the U.S.–Russian or Japanese–Russian Incidents at Sea agreements, broadened to include safety-at-sea measures.

(b) Broaden the substantial existing cooperation on nuclear safety. A large and growing nuclear energy industry exists in Northeast Asia, and throughout the larger region nuclear energy is viewed as a solution to growing energy demands. The region includes a number of world leaders on nuclear energy, such as Japan, South Korea, and Russia, while Taiwan is expanding its program and Indonesia and North Korea are pursuing plans to build reactors. China has the most ambitious nuclear develop-ment plan in the world. Nuclear power in Asia could surpass that in the West, both in terms of generating capacity and of exports and imports of nuclear technology.[11] Mutual interests in

the peaceful uses of nuclear energy provide opportunities for CSBMs, with early emphasis on joint measures focusing on nuclear safety. Few issues of civil policy are so fraught with long-term security considerations.

Regional measures might begin first in Northeast Asia and expand elsewhere in the region as others put nuclear industries in place. All of the countries with nuclear programs in Asia are parties to the NPT and members of the International Atomic Energy Agency (IAEA). Yet there are concerns about nuclear safety throughout the region. Peaceful nuclear CSBMs could address a wide range of safety issues such as nuclear waste; radiation exposure and protection standards; implementing the international nuclear safety convention; accident warning and liability; emergency accident response; operator training; and the establishment of nuclear regulatory agencies. A model for such regional cooperation is the 1994 Japan-South Korea-Russia joint study of radioactive contamination of the North Pacific. Such projects might be conducted under IAEA auspices. Related proposals are presented under recommendation number 4.

(c) Strengthen systems of national export control and expand international cooperation.   The nations of the Asia Pacific have not been as aggressive as their counterparts in the Organization for Economic Cooperation and Development (OECD) in adapting their export controls to the new international conditions of the 1990s. After the scandals associated with arms sales to Iraq in the 1980s, and in the wake of the collapse of the Soviet Union, OECD members working in a variety of formal and informal coordinating mechanisms have worked to strengthen their cooperation on export controls and to redefine the tasks of export controls in the new era. As industrializing countries in the Asia Pacific emerge as producers of military technology and of dual-use technologies of concern, especially in the area of weapons of mass destruction, the character of the controls over associated exports becomes more important. The region's technological dynamism and the independence of its private sector suggest that existing export control mechanisms will be overwhelmed by existing trends. Failure to effectively control indigenous technologies—or to prevent the reexport of U.S.-provided technologies—would deepen the trade frictions that already resonate across the Pacific.

Exporters within the region of the technologies necessary for the production of nuclear, biological, and chemical weapons and missile delivery systems are encouraged to seek membership in the relevant export coordinating mechanism (Zangger Committee, Australia Group, and Missile Technology Control Regime [MTCR]). The emergence of China alone as a supplier of dual-use technology could make or break international efforts to regulate trade in these areas; its nuclear export record is a source of concern within and outside the region. Yet China is not a member of the Nuclear Suppliers Group (NSG); it should become one. China should also be included in whatever export control mechanism emerges in the wake of the demise of the Coordinating Committee for Multilateral Export Controls (CoCom) in early 1994. The process of forging a new consensus on nuclear and dual-use export controls could serve as an important CSBM. Japan, a member of the NSG, could be instrumental in such a process.

3. Proceed with New Multilateral Approaches to Current Regional Conflicts, But Do so Cautiously

The task force notes the enthusiasm that has been heard in some quarters for multilateral security dialogues focused on hot spots in the region. We believe that the timing is not now right for a substantial shift in the diplomatic agenda in either Northeast Asia or on the Spratly Islands, because such a shift might well generate both resistance and the opposite of confidence. On the other hand, events may move in ways that would give such forums a constructive role in managing regional conflicts. Thus, work in this direction should be continued with an eye on the mid- to long term.

In North Korea, for example, it is important that the focus on short-term concerns not distract us completely from the longer-term challenge of facilitating Korean reunification and the subsequent emergence of a united Korea in the region. An informal or low-key dialogue on the future of Northeast Asian security should be encouraged; the dialogue would serve as a CSBM in itself while also helping to identify more concrete CSBMs that might be adopted in a changed context. In this regard, we endorse the recommendations for a regional security dialogue made by the South Korean foreign minister at the July 1994 ARF meeting.

With regard to the Spratly Islands, China's strong preference for handling the negotiations on a bilateral basis cannot now be reversed. This does not preclude, however, an informal dialogue, such as that spurred by Indonesia, to identify problems and possibilities should short-term constraints give way in the medium or long term. In order to raise the visibility of this work, it would be useful to invite Indonesia to report regularly to the ARF on its progress. It would also be useful to identify specific measures, such as a unilateral moratorium on economic development and military construction in the South China Seas, that would build confidence that parties to the conflict seek a negotiated solution.

4. Support Global Arms Control Treaty Regimes

Nations of the Asia Pacific can and should do more in support of global arms control treaty regimes because of the benefits of confidence and security they bring to the region. As noted earlier, one of the primary concerns of the USCSCAP CSBM task force is the potential in the region in future decades for unconventional weapons proliferation and for arms races and their attendant instabilities. We recognize that many in the Asia Pacific do not share the sense of urgency about this problem that prevails in the United States. Part of our purpose in making these recommendations is to stimulate debate about the problem.

The current concern has three sources. First, although short-term pressures for proliferation in the region are limited, long-term pressures are not as easily discounted. The diffusion of dual-use technology and of an advanced defense industrial base across the region raises questions about whether some states might quietly be assembling the means to create such weapons in future crises—questions that erode confidence about the long-term stability of relations among states in the region. Second, although the legitimate right of all states to self-defense and the goal of modernization may drive most conventional weapons acquisition programs within the region, history is rife with armaments programs that became competitive and resulted in destabilizing arms races. Third, a particular urgency attaches to strengthening the global treaty regimes at this time.

The years 1995 and 1996 will be critical in determining the future of these regimes in the wake of the great geopolitical changes of the last decade and the revelations about treaty noncompliance in Iraq and North Korea. During this time, a conference will be convened to review and possibly extend the NPT; another conference will be convened to consider measures to strengthen compliance with the BWC; the Chemical Weapons

Convention (CWC) will either enter into force or slip rapidly from the world scene; and a conference will be held to consider a comprehensive nuclear test ban. In this time of trial for the global treaty regimes, the active support of states in the Asia Pacific takes on special importance. Put conversely, their failure to offer such support at a time of uncertainty within the region and in light of their existing technical competence would cast further doubt on the legitimacy and durability of these treaties.

Whatever the different transpacific perceptions of the problem, we believe that it is possible at this time to reach agreement on a number of constructive steps.

*(a) **Work immediately toward full participation in existing treaties.*** Over recent decades the international community has put in place a number of global treaties: the Nuclear Non-Proliferation Treaty and associated safeguards treaties, the Biological and Toxin Weapons Convention, the new Chemical Weapons Convention, and the United Nations Register of Conventional Arms. As regimes, they embody agreed norms, moderate the behavior of states capable of building such weapons, and form the basis of expectations that egregious noncompliance will be punished. When states fail to participate fully in these regimes, questions arise about the exact nature of their intent: Does weak participation convey opposition to the purposes of the regime and an intent to cheat, or merely oversight?

The record of participation by states of the Asia Pacific in these global treaty regimes is not what it should be. The pattern of uneven and incomplete participation nourishes the fear that the region may well succumb to widespread proliferation of weapons of mass destruction and other high-leverage weapons. This pattern also deepens doubt about the future effectiveness of these regimes at a time when such doubts are firmly in place as a result of extant proliferation and the crises of proliferation in Iraq, North Korea, and Ukraine, among other places.

With regard to the NPT, the regional lineup was strengthened with China's accession, but a critical gap remains with respect to North Korea, as well as larger gaps in the safeguards system. Of particular concern is the emergence of a number of new suppliers of nuclear technologies—itself not something forbidden by the NPT but nonetheless a cause for concern. Moreover, few states in the region have taken an active role in seeking the extension of the NPT when its fate is considered at a special conference in April 1995; some greater activism on this question would help quell doubts about a region with noteworthy pressures for proliferation.

With regard to the BWC, a number of important holdouts remain. But the more important pattern of nonparticipation relates to the series of confidence building measures adopted at recent review conferences for the treaty: by 1991, only 41 of the more than 130 states that are parties to the treaty globally had participated in the adopted measures, raising questions about willful obfuscation or simple lack of interest in the problems of biological weapons and their proliferation. In 1993, only 5 Asia Pacific countries—China, Japan, the Republic of Korea, Australia, and New Zealand—submitted the requested data.

With regard to the CWC, which has not yet entered into force, there are many signatories (as well as some important nonsignatories) in the region but virtually no states that have deposited their instruments of ratification with the UN. Members of the European Union have made a commitment to ratify as a group and to be members of the convention when it enters into force. Analogous efforts in the Asia Pacific to secure early entry into force of the CWC, to encourage full participation and compliance by states in the region, and to support the interim work of the Preparatory Commission with fiscal and political resources would ease doubts about the future relevance of the new regime for the region—and give the CWC an important fillip.

With regard to the UN Arms Register, most states in the region participated during the first year (1993). But some major importers of weapons such as Thailand and Taiwan did not report on imports (the latter perhaps only because it is not a member of the UN). North Korea, a major exporter, did not report. China, another major exporter, reported with minimal data and provided none of the background material relevant to its declarations (unlike many other countries). The register is defined specifically as a mechanism for "the building of confidence and security, the reduction of suspicions, mistrust and fear, restraint on a unilateral and multilateral basis, and the timely identification of trends in arms transfers"[12] and accordingly merits the full participation of states committed to CSBMs in the region.

These global measures are important because they provide reassurance to states that their neighbors are not about to embark on new weapons programs of strategic significance. They have other benefits for the region as well. One of the principal benefits is the effect that full Chinese participation would have in making its military establishment and ambitions more transparent. They also bring some economic benefits, insofar as they are an alternative to efforts to constrain proliferation that focus on export controls and so-called strategies of denial that, over time, could seriously limit trade in dual-use technologies while aggravating trade relations more generally.

In the longer term, it would be useful to discuss within the region either membership of the Open Skies Treaty or creation of an analogous regional mechanism.

(b) A regional organization to oversee the nuclear fuel cycle, akin to the European Atomic Energy Community (EURATOM), should be constructed. This would supplement but go well beyond the nuclear safety cooperation measures discussed in an earlier section. The global nuclear nonproliferation regime is intended to provide a degree of assurance through its associated safeguards mechanisms that the long-term risk of nuclear weaponization does not accompany the development of civilian nuclear industries. In the Asia Pacific, where reliance on nuclear energy for electricity generation is considerable, the degree of assurance provided by the global mechanisms is no longer sufficient. In both China and Japan—as elsewhere in the region—spent or recycled nuclear materials are now accumulating. Japan's policy of recovering plutonium from spent reactor fuel is a source of concern, as is North Korea's plutonium inventory. A regional approach to the nuclear fuel cycle would ease concerns about national policies by storing and/or disposing of nuclear waste under international safeguards. Such a regional authority might also oversee the mining, purchase, enrichment, and fabrication of nuclear fuel at the front end of the fuel cycle.

These tasks, like those mentioned in recommendation (1), could be addressed in a forum modeled after EURATOM, Europe's nuclear agency. As a CSBM, an Asian atomic energy community (ASIATOM) could facilitate functional cooperation in areas of mutual interest and mutual concern. ASIATOM could oversee a wide range of activities by augmenting existing IAEA safeguards with its own regional safeguards system, specially tailored to satisfy regional requirements. In addition to nonproliferation, safety, and fuel cycle cooperation, ASIATOM might consider a regional or subregional electric power grid that could provide energy to countries such as North Korea where confidence about nuclear intentions is low.

(c) Target discretionary funds to IAEA enforcement actions.
Looking beyond the immediate crisis in North Korea, and
assuming extension of the NPT in April 1995, it will be important
to bolster the function of the IAEA safeguards system if the credibility of the nuclear nonproliferation regime is to be preserved—
and indeed improved—after the crises in the Middle East and
East Asia. One means of doing this would be to help the IAEA
survive the fiscal crisis imposed by having to operate within a
fixed budget even as its tasks multiply. Given the fixed pattern of
allocations within the IAEA, nearly 90 percent of all monies
given to the IAEA go toward nuclear assistance programs, and
not enforcement activities. But it is possible to target assistance
toward these discretionary accounts.

The long-term interest of all states in the region in preventing
nuclearization points to the virtue of using some tiny portion of
their accumulating wealth to buttress the principal instrument of
the international community in catching nuclear cheaters. A
regionwide commitment to increase national contributions to the
IAEA for enforcement activities in the Asia Pacific would be particularly welcome.

*(d) The United States should sign the protocol of the South
Pacific Nuclear Free Zone (SPNFZ).*   Nuclear-weapons-free zones
in Latin America and Antarctica and the ocean floor have proven
a useful adjunct to the global nuclear nonproliferation regime
and a new such zone is likely in Africa within the year. The traditional reluctance of the United States concerning such zones, and
particularly the SPNFZ, has passed with the end of the cold war.
The United States should accede to the Treaty of Rarotonga, recognizing that it accommodates U.S. interests including the "neither confirm nor deny" policy and the right to transit, because of
the important nonproliferation and confidence building benefits
it offers. We recognize, however, the importance of proceeding
toward accession in a manner consistent with the broader goal of
negotiating a global comprehensive test ban.

Dialogue within the region should also continue on other
such zones. We call attention to the consensus among the major
powers in Northeast Asia regarding the advantages of a nuclear-
free zone on the Korean peninsula and urge progress toward that
goal. We also note the discussions about a possible nuclear-
weapons-free zone in Southeast Asia and encourage our counterparts in the U.S. government to join those discussions with a
clear awareness of the way in which cold war realities shaped

past U.S. predispositions in this area. We also wish to enjoin Asian diplomats to be more open about their thinking and work on this subject with the nuclear weapon states with interests in the region.

5. Promote a Dialogue on Effective Governance

This task force recognizes the sometimes corrosive impact of the debate about human rights on transpacific relations and recommends the creation of nongovernmental and multilateral mechanisms to promote a dialogue on effective governance to deal with this contentious issue. We also recognize that U.S. enthusiasm to promote this dialogue is not necessarily shared elsewhere in the region.

Rather than engage in transpacific polemical exchanges, we desire to channel the debate toward more productive possibilities. Communities regionwide are all struggling with shared problems of civil society and democratic culture in modernizing societies. Each of our societies is trying to find the balance between individual and group rights, between political and economic rights, between the family and society, and between spiritual and material values. We recognize the process of building a democratic society, of preserving inherited values, and of defining the necessary ingredients of effective governance is an unending one. We desire a quality of dialogue within our transpacific community that enriches this discussion, one conducted in a spirit of mutual openness. Toward that end, we propose the following:

(a) Speakers programs and other programs of educational exchange should be created that will open up currents of thinking in the region for broader understanding. The U.S. government has created programs specifically to ensure that the currents of American society and the leaders of American opinion are understood abroad. These include, for example, the Fulbright scholarships and the speakers programs of the United States Information Agency that bring visitors to the United States and send U.S. citizens abroad. Regional adaptations should be created.

(b) Patterns of cooperation among states should be deepened to include many elements of the democratic polity. Programs to promote parliamentary cooperation, regional associations of jurists,

and broader civil-military and military-to-military contacts should be developed. In Europe and Latin America, these have proven to be bulwarks against international uncertainty.

(c) A regional nongovernmental institution should be established and funded by states in the region that promotes political pluralism and the building up of civil society.   In Germany, the foundations established by the political parties have been instrumental in nurturing Germany's democratic revolution and reaching out to like-minded politicians in other countries to train them in democratic procedures and institutions. In the United States, the National Endowment for Democracy has funneled funds through American institutions to train and equip democrats in many countries. Former president Jimmy Carter's center at Emory University has played an important role in facilitating the process of bargaining and compromise necessary in all political communities. These analogues should find regional adaptations in the Asia Pacific. The fledgling Asia Pacific Parliamentary Forum illustrates the regional possibilities. In particular, we believe that such an institution might be empowered to provide international supervision of elections, to assist with the professionalization of political parties, and to assist with programs of civic education.

Defining a Strategy

If debate in the coming years begins to coalesce around this agenda and some or all of the steps are implemented, we believe the foundations will have been set in place for the future achievement of a real Security Community in the Asia Pacific—so long as relations among the major powers maintain some semblance of balance. But it will not be possible to do everything at once, and it is necessary to make some choices within this overall agenda of basic priorities. We think the following priorities make the most sense.

Top priority should go to carrying forward the current ARF process expeditiously. A broad agenda could be quickly implemented with positive effect, so long as clearly defined measures are linked to well-defined problems. Through this incremental approach the sense of community and structures of cooperation in the region will gradually grow stronger. It is necessary that ARF be ambitious enough to do more than the merely simple, so that—in the process of accomplishing something where there is some minor risk of failure or difficulty—it does, in fact, generate some confidence for itself. Hence our earlier admonition against initiatives too ambitious or unrealistic at this time.

Our second priority is the full participation of the Asia Pacific in existing global mechanisms. People in the region do not perhaps realize the important benefits this could bring.

Third, we would like to work toward an expansion of the CSBM approach into other subregions of the Asia Pacific. This will be a gradual process, but given the rapid pace of change in the region, we can reasonably expect that the terms of debate will have shifted decisively in one way or another in the years ahead, and that we will be debating new proposals for new measures throughout the region.

We have attempted to sketch out an agenda that is both pragmatic and visionary—one that looks both to the desirable and the possible. We believe that the security of states in the Asia Pacific would be well served by a rapid embrace of this agenda. Failure to do so today could well compel officials to tackle much more difficult tasks of confidence and security building a decade or two hence—if not sooner.

Notes

1.　We note particularly, the ARF statement of July 25, 1994, detailing a set of studies to be conducted in support of future ASEAN action.

2.　As Desmond Ball has observed, "Transparency is not a neutral strategic value. The effect of transparency is different for countries with more 'defensive' as opposed to 'offensive' defense postures, as well as for those countries more dependent upon arms imports rather than indigenous production. It can expose vulnerabilities (in both intelligence collection and force structure capabilities). Uncertainty about the capabilities of potential adversaries sometimes serves to enhance deterrence (or to induce caution)." See Ball, "Arms and Affluence: Military Acquisitions in the Asia-Pacific Region," *International Security* 18, no. 3 (winter 1993/94): 108.

3.　See the taxonomy and overview of CSBMs prepared in support of this project by Susan Pederson and Stanley Weeks and contained in chapter 5 of this volume.

4.　See, for example, the taxonomies of regional security challenges addressed in chapters 2 through 4 of this volume.

5.　As Barry Buzan and Gerald Segal have argued, going "back to the future is a distinct possibility in Asia." See Buzan and Segal, "Rethinking East Asian Security," *Survival* 36, no. 2 (summer 1994): 3–21; and the collection of essays in Robert S. Ross, *East Asia in Transition: Toward a New Regional Order* (forthcoming).

6.   For a discussion of this particular contribution of ASEAN to the original member countries, see Michael Antolik, *ASEAN and the Diplomacy of Accommodation* (Armonk, N.Y.: M. E. Sharpe, 1990).

7.   Chairman's Statement, The First Meeting of the ASEAN Regional Forum (ARF), July 25, 1994, Bangkok.

8.   See Ro-Myung Gong, "The Consequences of Arms Proliferation in Asia: I," and Gerald Segal, "The Consequences of Arms Proliferation: II," in "Asia's International Role in the Post–Cold War Era, Part II," conference papers, *Adelphi Paper* no. 276 (London: Brassey's for IISS, 1993); and Gerald Segal, "Managing New Arms Races in the Asia-Pacific," *The Washington Quarterly* 15, no. 3 (summer 1992). As Desmond Ball has reported, from 1982 to 1991 the combination of Asia's increased defense spending and the decline elsewhere resulted in a doubling of Asia's share of global defense spending while its share of global arms imports more than doubled to 34 percent in 1991. See Ball, "Trends in Military Acquisitions in the Region: Implications for Constraints and Controls," *Reference Paper* no. 192 (The Strategic and Defence Studies Centre, The Research School of Pacific Studies, The Australian National University, Canberra, June 1993). Increased arms acquisitions do not necessarily mean that the Asia Pacific is today caught up in arms race behavior: "Although the countries of East Asia are not engaged in an arms race in the sense of a frantic increase in spending on arms, the combination of falling arms imports and gradually rising defence spending in the region suggests that the trend is towards a gradual proliferation of locally-produced weapons. . . . Defence spending by most ASEAN states is down as a percentage of GDP . . . and arms imports have essentially been flat for a decade . . . the upshot is cycles among ASEAN states that are no longer synchronised, thus feeding regional paranoias." IISS, *Strategic Survey 1993–94* (London: Brassey's for IISS, 1994), 41–45.

9.   See Douglas M. Johnston, "Anticipating Instability in the Asia-Pacific," *The Washington Quarterly* 15, no. 3 (summer 1992). On ASEAN bilateral military exercises, see Amitav Acharya, "A New Regional Order in South-East Asia: ASEAN in the Post–Cold War Era" *Adelphi Paper* no. 279 (London: Brassey's for IISS, 1993), 70–71.

10.   W.S.G. Bateman, "Multinational Naval Cooperation—A Pacific View" (paper for a conference on "Multinational Naval Cooperation" held at the Royal Naval Staff College, Greenwich, United Kingdom, December 12–13, 1991).

11.   *Outlook on Asian Nuclear Power,* special report to the readers of *Nucleonics Week, Inside N.R.C. and Nuclear Fuel,* June/July 1994.

12.   *Study on Ways and Means of Promoting Transparency in International Transfers of Conventional Arms,* UN General Assembly document A/47/301, September 9, 1991, p. 37. See also Edward J. Laurance, Siemon T. Wezeman, and Herbert Wulf, *Arms Watch: SIPRI Report on the First Year of the UN Register of Conventional Arms,* SIPRI Research Report no. 6 (Oxford: Oxford University Press for SIPRI, 1994).

CSIS Books of Related Interest

Asian Values and the United States: How Much Conflict?

David I. Hitchcock

The reassertion of Asian cultures and values and the proposal that Asian cultures have a strong kinship have emerged as spirited topics of discussion. To what extent is this thinking prompted by reaction to Western influences perceived to be divisive to Western societies? Or to what extent does this thinking stem from internal desires to give new attention to the indigenous cultural and spiritual side of modern life? This timely book addresses "cultural determinants" in international affairs.

CSIS *Report*   41 pp.   1994
ISBN 0-89206-311-4 $10.95

❖   ❖   ❖

China's Conventional Military Capabilities, 1994–2004: An Assessment

John Caldwell

China's growing military budget and acquisition of advanced military equipment have raised concerns in various countries in Asia. Some Asian observers argue, however, that China's military modernization program is unlikely to pose much of a regional threat. First, China is focused on economic development, and, second, Beijing is merely replacing obsolete hardware with a limited quantity of modern equipment. This report examines these divergent views and evaluates China's military modernization program and its potential impact on regional security.

CSIS *Report*   28 pp.   1994
ISBN 0-89206-257-6 $14.95

❖   ❖   ❖

Korean Unification: Implications for Northeast Asia

Amos A. Jordan, editor

Contributors: Chen Qimao, Gerrit W. Gong, Amos A. Jordan, Seo-Hang Lee, Masao Okonogi, Young-Kyu Park, Li Sam Ro, and Sergei Rogov

Experts from China, Japan, the United States, North and South Korea, and Russia assess the differing approaches to unification adopted by Pyongyang and Seoul. The authors examine the political, economic, and strategic dimensions of the unification process, as well as the regional implications of unification itself for Northeast Asia.

Significant Issues Series   120 pp.   1993
ISBN 0-89206-215-0 $16.00

❖   ❖   ❖

Ratifying the Chemical Weapons Convention

Brad Roberts, editor

Contributors: Kathleen Bailey, Walter Busbee, Will Carpenter, Anthony Cordesman, John Gee, Elisa Harris, John Holum, Karen Jansen, Sergei Kisselev, Martin Lancaster, Donald Mahley, Matthew Meselson, Robert Mikulak, Michael Moodie, Brad Roberts, Amy Smithson

This volume begins with an update on the work of the Preparatory Commission and continues with an assessment of U.S. preparations for the implementation phase. The main focus, however, is the set of chapters evaluating the merits and drawbacks of the Convention in terms of U.S. national interests.

Significant Issues Series   126 pp.   1994
ISBN 0-89206-264-9 $13.50

❖   ❖   ❖

Security Cooperation in the Asia-Pacific Region
Desmond Ball, Richard L. Grant, and Jusuf Wanandi

The debate under way in Asia over the future of regional security is focusing on multilateral consultation and cooperation. Multilateralism is increasingly viewed as the most effective means for resolving long-standing tensions and addressing the new security issues in the region. This volume assesses that approach and includes the statement of commitment to CSCAP—Council for Security Cooperation in the Asia Pacific—launched in summer 1993.

Significant Issues Series   38 pp.   1993
ISBN 0-89206-219-3 $8.50

❖   ❖   ❖

U.S. China Policy: Building a New Consensus
Gerrit Gong, editor

Contributors: A. Doak Barnett, Jim Kolbe, Max Baucus, Donald E. Russell, E. Barrie Wiggham, Robert F. Bennett, Alan K. Simpson, David D. Dreier, David E. Skaggs

In the twenty-first century, a key challenge for international society will be to incorporate China as a full, responsible, and constructive member. Finding an answer to this fundamental issue—taking into account developments on the ground in the PRC, in a wider China area, in East and Southeast Asia, and by fixing U.S. interests, vital and otherwise, including values and desires—is the challenge of defining the new consensus in U.S. China policy.

Asian Studies Report   105 pp.   1994
ISBN 0-89206-303-3 $12.95

❖   ❖   ❖

Weapons Proliferation in the 1990s
Brad Roberts, editor

The proliferation of weapons of mass destruction has
emerged as a major topic of international security in the
post-cold war world. This volume offers fresh thinking about
the proliferation subject and the changing policy agenda. It
describes the changing nature of the problem in the 1990s,
discusses new trends in nonproliferation and counterprolifer-
ation policy, identifies new arms control challenges at the
regional and global levels, and concludes with a discussion of
the global politics of proliferation.

Copublished Book / MIT Press   Forthcoming   July 1995

❖   ❖   ❖

For information on these and other CSIS publications, contact:

CSISBOOKS
1800 K Street, N.W.
Washington, D.C.   20006
Telephone   202-775-3119
Facsimile   202-775-3199